GOOD GRIEF

GOOD

How to recover from grief, loss or a broken heart

GRIEF

Zita Annette Weber PhD

mg

Published by
Margaret Gee
PO Box 221, Double Bay NSW 1360, Australia
Tel: (02) 9365 3266   Fax: (02) 9365 3168

First published 2001

National Library of Australia Cataloguing-in-Publication entry
Weber, Zita Annette
Good grief:
how to recover from grief, loss or a broken heart

ISBN   1 875574 40 9

Design and print management
Reno Design Group, Sydney   R21005
Designer Graham Rendoth
Printing Griffin Press
Distribution Gary Allen Pty Ltd, Sydney
Publishing manager Sardine Waters

In memory of my father, Laszlo Weber
21 February 1927 – 28 March 2001

CONTENTS

AUTHOR'S THANKS

My thanks go to Margaret Gee for her enormous and continuing encouragement of my work and to Dr Brent Waters for his support.

Thank you again, John.

ACKNOWLEDGMENTS

The author acknowledges the work of the following authors, whose scales, exercises and ideas have helped shape her own:

- Glassock and Rowling, 1992
- Grollman and Kosik, 1996
- Levang, 1998
- McBride, 1996
- McKissock, 1983
- J. William Worden, 1991

INTRODUCTION

I first experienced a personal loss when I was too young to understand. I felt profoundly unhappy and I even became physically ill, but I didn't have the words to articulate what my body and soul felt – grief. I was heart-broken. My loss was related to migration. I was losing my place of birth, my language, my heritage, and most importantly of all, my grandparents. I was particularly close to my maternal grandmother, and moving country meant leaving her behind. My parents were migrating – and I was going with them. As with most loss, the situation was not of my choosing.

My life has been punctuated by loss. By losses of all sorts. Some of these losses were easier to bear than others. I have attempted to work through these losses – and even learn and grow from each experience. My working life has also involved loss – listening to losses experienced by others, and helping them cope in their own way with these losses. I've sat with people in rooms filled with memories and images of past loss. In rooms where people talked and talked and cried and cried about their losses.

Each of us copes differently with our losses. However, by listening to each other, and learning from our collective experiences, we each become more individually empowered.

Grief is the pain of loss. Grief is a state of distress associated with different types of loss. Grief is an inner psychological experience in response to loss. It is possible for people to hide this experience from themselves. Sometimes, it's just too hard to confront the enormity of the situation – and the depth of the pain. In grief, it's easy to turn to the dubious comforts of alcohol and drugs – and to drive the pain away. At least for a while.

Distancing ourselves from the psychological pain can end up in expressing our distress in physical symptoms. Often these symptoms can be just annoying, but at times, they can masquerade as more serious illness.

Once a client whom I was seeing for counselling observed, *'It would be good if there was a pill for grief. Can't someone come up with a pill that will take away the sorrow and give me a sense of peace?'*

This client is not alone in her wish for some magical relief, without the pain of experiencing the sorrow. But, in reality, there is no machine to drain away all the sorrow, nor is there a laser treatment to correct the pain. Most importantly, there is no quick-fix when it comes to grief.

In fact, it might be said that the chemical calm afforded by drugs might impede the working through of our grief. It is understandable that people would like to avoid the pain, but 'good grief' will mean recovery, growth and change.

The wounded heart needs attention. The grieving heart needs time to mend and heal, and to strengthen. However, time alone, is not enough to heal the wounds of the heart. There is work involved in grieving.

Grieving is not easy. To express our sadness may seem a most natural life experience. Yet, we live in a society that sometimes wants to deny that loss and change can be disruptive and grieving might threaten the hope of eternal happiness.

It is important to understand that grief-work – understanding your grief, resolving your grief – and moving on – helps to empower you. Grieving is a healing process. Good grief leads to good health.

This book presents a practical approach. A practical approach that offers discussion and some ideas about how to cope with the complexity of emotions that comprise grief. Importantly, this book acknowledges the importance of giving permission to grieve, a reassurance that grieving and withdrawal from the world in order to regenerate, is normal. It gives permission to feel the pervasive sense of sadness and loss.

You will read about other people's stories of coping with loss and grief and how they moved on with their lives. You will be given information to help you make sense of your experience and tasks to encourage you to be active in your grief-work. You will be encouraged to read and write through your grief. You will gain a greater understanding of how you can cope with your loss and move forward with your life. Your self-awareness will be heightened and your coping strategies strengthened.

Loss is part of our daily life. The grieving process also is part of our daily life. From loss, through grief, we move towards adaptation and a renewed sense of coherence in daily life. 'Good grief' provides people with the opportunity of leaving behind the past with its losses and moving forward to the present with its potential gains.

PART I

THE SHADOWS OF LOSS

'Is there no pity sitting in the clouds,
That sees into the bottom of my grief?'

WILLIAM SHAKESPEARE [Romeo and Juliet]

1

LOSS AND GRIEF:
PART OF OUR DAILY LIFE

'It was on Good Friday that Miss Bendix lost her faith.
She had really lost it before then, but, as is often the case with losses, she did not
notice that anything was missing for some time after it had gone.'

NAOMI ROYDE-SMITH [Miss Bendix, 1938]

Changes and losses occur during our lifetimes. They are sometimes expected, often unwanted and usually unwelcome. We might feel as if we've been dealt a duff hand, but learning skills and strategies to help us in our loss can ensure that the grieving process will proceed normally, and we will achieve 'good grief'. Learning how to use 'good grief' to our advantage is very powerful in helping us to cope.

Grieving can be a long and arduous journey. Doing grief-work ensures that you will move from disorganisation to reorganisation and from pain to gain. As with most work, in grief-work, your rewards depend on the amount of effort you put into the process of healing yourself to face life after loss.

How do we begin to understand the turning-point that is loss? How do we learn to ease the pain of grief? Perhaps examining an old Jewish story is our starting point. Called ***The first tear***, it poetically expresses loss, grief and adaptation.

The first tear

'After Adam and Eve were driven out of the Garden of Eden, God saw their repentance. He felt pity for them and said, "Poor children! I have punished you for your transgressions and have driven you out of the Garden of Eden, where you lived without worry and grief. Now you are entering a world full of unhappiness and grief. But you shall come to know that I am generous and that my love for you is infinite. I know that in the world you will encounter much adversity and it will sadden your lives. Therefore, I shall bestow upon you my most precious treasure, the costly pearl – the tear. When your hearts are about to break, the pain becomes unbearable and grief overwhelms you, then this tear will fall from your eyes, and immediately, the burden will be easier to bear."

'Hearing these words, Adam and Eve became numb with grief. Tears welled up in their eyes and streamed down their cheeks. Their tears fell upon the earth.

'It was these tears of pain which first moistened the earth. And so Adam and Eve left behind a precious inheritance to their children. Ever since that first tear fell, when someone is in pain and feels great grief, tears flow from his eyes. And behold! The grief eases.'

From this story we come to understand that the recognition of the loss, the feelings that follow and the tears that result, can lead to a renewed sense of ease. This story is symbolic. Adam and Eve began their new life with loss.

LEARNING ABOUT ATTACHMENT AND LOSS

Judith Viorst, in **Necessary Losses**, begins by saying:

'We begin with loss. We are cast from the womb without an apartment, a charge plate, a job or a car.'

Confronting as these sentences are, they are nevertheless, true. Judith Viorst points out that loss begins within the first moments of life, and continues unabated through childhood and follows us into every aspect of our adulthood. Her thesis is that these losses are painful but they are necessary. Necessary losses are the high cost of living a meaningful life.

Judith Viorst says:

> 'Our losses include not only our separations and departures from those we love, but our conscious and unconscious losses of romantic dreams, impossible expectations, illusions of freedom and power, illusions of safety – and the loss of our own younger self, the self that thought it would always be unwrinkled and invulnerable and immortal.'

Loss, in its many forms, is a fact of life. Rabbi Harold Kushner rightly pointed out that – bad things do happen to good people. Grief visits us all. And when it does, life seems to lose its meaning. However, a satisfying and meaningful life is possible after loss – if our grief is resolved.

For successful resolution to occur, some basic assumptions and ways of being in the world are challenged. First, loss can challenge our closely held assumptions of personal invulnerability. Most of us know that bad things happen but we may believe that they happen to other people. Secondly, loss challenges an assumption that the world is meaningful and just and that things happen for a good reason. Thirdly, loss challenges our assumption that if we are 'good' people and 'play by the rules' then bad things will not happen to us.

Some losses may violate more greatly these assumptions than others. Generally speaking, the 'greater' the loss, the greater the violation of our assumptions about the world and our place in it.

We may begin with loss, but paradoxically, we also learn attachment very early in life. When attachment is threatened or when attachment between people or between people and something important to them is interrupted – they feel as sense of loss.

John Bowlby, the famous English psychiatrist, developed a theory around attachment and loss. He believed that by the end of the first year, most infants have usually developed a strong attachment to their parents – particularly to their mothers. Close attachment is as important to the infant as food and drink.

Attachment behaviour is crucial for the infant's survival. It encourages the child to maintain contact with those around him or her who appear able to cope with the world.

In the face of possible danger, the infant feels more secure in being close to its mother. Studies have shown that when faced with threatened or actual separation from its mother, the child becomes anxious and demonstrates its wish to be close to her. Attachment, therefore, ensures that the child has a secure base from which to explore the world.

Attachment can grow throughout the months and years of the child's life – but this ability to attach – to establish relationships and closeness with other people appears to be present from birth.

Interestingly, researchers have found that it takes about 36 months for a child to feel and behave psychologically as if she or he were an individual in their own right – separate from their mother. At that point, the child learns that she or he is not merely an extension of the mother. However, to cope with this early separation experience, the child often turns to what is called a 'transitional object' or 'security blanket' as evidenced in Linus's blanket (from the **Peanuts** comic strip). For some children, this security blanket is soft, such as a pillow, teddy bear or blanket – and it is recognisable by its odour. Typically, this security blanket is held for solace when the child is feeling vulnerable or at bed-time. For most children, this transitional object they have become attached to is a normal stage of development and their particular security blanket is discarded when it's no longer needed.

TO HAVE AND HAVE NOT

Infants need nourishment, warmth and comfort. If these needs are not met, the baby protests loudly. We carry this early 'have and have not' principle with us into childhood and adulthood. We all develop a set of assumptions and expectations that certain people will be there and certain things will happen. When any of our attachments are broken, we discover loss.

For very young children who don't yet understand words, loss and change can make them very vulnerable. It is impossible to explain to an infant or toddler that mummy is in hospital, but will return soon or that the child itself will be in hospital for a few days for its own good. Young children exist in a world where they 'have or have not' – either their needs are met – or they are not met.

However, children do learn about loss by experimenting with loss through game-playing. Hide-and-seek and peek-a-boo allow children to begin learning that nothing ever stays quite the same in life. Children learn that people can go away and come back. Such temporary loss is also experienced by children who are separated from their mothers, or their 'mothering' source. We have all witnessed small children crying when parted from their source of mothering. Some will cry until the 'mother' returns. Researchers have found that if the loss continues then children can become depressed. The patterns of crying and even screaming will give way to a withdrawn kind of behaviour. This withdrawn behaviour, for example, sitting quietly in the corner may be mistaken for settled behaviour or 'good behaviour'. In fact, the child is grieving the temporary loss.

All sorts of minor losses are experienced in childhood. A best friend moves away to another city, a favourite toy goes missing, a special jumper or dress or pair of trousers becomes too small and is thrown away. There is also a sense of loss associated with moving away from everything that is familiar at pre-school to the strangeness of 'big school'.

Of course, not all of these losses will be experienced intensely. Some will create sadness and fear and others merely a passing regret. It is through such losses that we learn that nothing stays the same forever and that some losses are more quickly accepted than others.

Our attachment behaviour offers us completeness and protection in our lives. When we lose our attachment to someone or something, our safe world can become a frightening place. As everything we have known and relied upon is turned upside down, we temporarily lose our way in our lives.

FROM MINOR LOSS TO DEATH IS FOREVER

Although there is some dispute as to when a child will understand the concept of death, it is clear that the child given a clear and accurate explanation about death is at an advantage.

Life is full of death images – dead plants, insects, family pets and many images on television, including cartoons. Children will vary in their rate of development – and in their understanding. However, information about death which is hesitantly imparted or confusing, will lead to confusion for the child.

Some theorists believe that children are better able to understand and accept death than adults. Perhaps because children are busy learning new concepts every day, their minds are unclouded by the assumptions and expectations around what we believe and how we should behave. For children, information should be given simply, in a straight-forward manner.

When young children play 'Bang! Bang! You're Dead!' games, adults may believe that is proof that children don't understand death at all. Such games are experiments in new notions of power, with the children swapping roles and 'killing' each other. Perhaps through such games children are able to explore the complexity of the world in which they live and gradually learn how to cope with concepts like power, being out of control and death.

The learning continues for us all through childhood into adolescence and adulthood, with a range of possible losses: loss of some aspect of our identity, loss of expectations, loss of familiar surroundings, loss of a role or a job, separation and divorce. Each new situation of loss will teach us something further about the world in which we live – and ourselves.

THE LEARNING CONTINUES

So while we may be born with loss – and be forced to face the world without *an apartment, charge plate, a job or a car*', as Judith Viorst suggests, we also are born with an ability to attach to others. We also are born with the ability to learn to attach meaning to people and things in the world around us. If this meaning is important, then the attachment to the people or things becomes important.

This attachment behaviour can be transferred from one experience or situation to another. In this way, we learn from childhood, through adolescence into adulthood how to manage our life circumstances. Similar situations, or perceived similarities are put into familiar categories in our mind. So that the meanings we give to attachment and loss are transferable. So too are the consequences. The things that we have learnt.

Our lives are a series of makings and breakings of affectional bonds. Sometimes people report a 'searching' behaviour in the face of their affectional losses. On elderly woman, Dorothy, 78, told me that a recent loss of a friend had brought to mind for her a fear of memories long buried. She cried as she recalled the loss of her ten week old daughter, 58 years earlier. Her daughter had died of an infection, which had almost killed Dorothy as well. Dorothy said that her guilt and grief had not been expressed all those years ago. People around her said that the baby was so beautiful that God needed her more than she did. People said that it was God's will and that she should not cry nor be sad. People said she should not grieve and that she would soon have another child. In this respect, they were right. Dorothy did have another child within eighteen months, but she secretly never forgot about her daughter.

Dorothy spoke about how she has always remembered her daughter's birthdays, looked around her for girls, then women, of the right age and tried to imagine what her daughter would be like. Dorothy cried when she said she felt ashamed when for months after her daughter's death she would look in prams, searching for her dead baby. She knew her baby was dead, but it didn't stop Dorothy from searching for her. She was too embarrassed to tell her family and friends of her 'searching' behaviour, because they all wanted her to forget about her child.

Another woman, Beryl, 68, said that for about ten months after her husband's death, she would hear his keys in the front door at 6:15pm, see him in the garden, or sitting in his favourite chair and she continued to set a place for him at the dinner table.

Although seemingly irrational, when a major affectional bond is broken, some people try desperately to replace the missing person. Their rational mind tells them that 'searching' and 'seeing' their baby, their partner, or their parent is not possible, yet the remnants of their attachment result in such searches and sightings.

THE MEANING OF LOSS

Attachment, loss and adaptation to loss are part of the human experience. And it is from our experience that we learn to cope with the loss – we adapt to the loss as part of our journey towards recovery. It is not always obvious that this is happening. Often, we might think we have lost our way. We might fear that we'll never not feel a sense of loss and grief.

When we experience loss, we experience a break with an affinity to someone or something. We have lost an attachment. People can become attached to all sorts of things: human beings, expectations, jobs, prestige, money, home and other possessions. Often we take appearance and health for granted. However, when someone loses a breast or an arm or they become seriously ill, then they begin to understand the importance of their attachment to – and affinity with – their body. In this way, it becomes easy to recognise that when a person's attachment to someone or something is disrupted, and a loss ensues, then this triggers off the deepest grief.

In her book, ***Grief: The Mourning After***, Catherine M. Sanders, PhD, says the following about loss and grief:

> *'If we examine the typical life cycle of most Americans, we can reasonably expect that losses will occur to all of us for one reason for another. Yet, strangely, if not surprisingly, grief is denied by most until we are confronted head-on with a loss of our own. If we form attachments to family members, friends, spouses, homes, jobs, we will eventually have to relinquish that person or thing to whom the attachment was made. Letting go represents the ultimate pain of grief.'*

Our lives are full of losses – and feelings of grief. Grief can hurt so much – physically, emotionally and psychically. Letting go of someone or something dear to us is extremely painful. The insecurity we can feel after a loss is frightening.

While some losses hardly affect us, others can have long and painful effects that shadow us into the future.

For some of us, a major loss may visit early in childhood with, for instance, the death of a grandparent. Others of us seemingly escape significant loss experiences until our adulthood. However, all of us experience loss in smaller or larger ways. We are each unique. Each of us will have unique experiences. And as individuals, we all react differently.

Losses can occur on two levels: actual and symbolic. An actual loss occurs when a significant person dies, when we lose a body part, when we experience separation and divorce and when we lose our jobs.

A symbolic loss is generally related to an actual loss. For instance, when a man loses his job, much of his feeling of loss involves his sense of depleted ego identity. A job can define our role in life. Without the job, the solid sense of self that is attached to the role is lost. Another illustration is that involving death of a child. The grieving parent might see the child as an extension of herself. Symbolically, then, when the child dies, part of the parent dies as well.

WHAT ARE LIFE LOSSES?

A life loss is one that causes a change in our lives. These life losses range from the most obvious one, like a death, to less tangible and abstract losses like loss of trust, innocence, hopes and dreams and expectations. Note that the latter losses are symbolic ones.

Recently, it has been recognised that events like divorce and miscarriage also provoke strong grief reactions in us. But other types of losses also take their toll: losing a job, losing a friendship, infertility, failing memory and loss of independence can all cause us to grieve.

Sometimes it's hard for people to understand how seemingly positive events like travelling, getting married, starting a new job or moving home voluntarily can be felt like a form of loss. Loss, change and grief are interconnected.

Any change we experience contains the potential for loss – and growth. Not recognising a loss can become a source of stress. However, if the loss is accepted, the feelings of grief become accessible to us and the state of stress we feel can be resolved.

Recognising the connection between loss and change means we can understand why so many people are puzzled about their feelings of disappointment and lack of joy at times when they believe they ought to be experiencing much joy and sense of satisfaction.

Being promoted, completing a difficult task, getting married, having children, changing jobs, retiring are all examples of times when there are changes which entail invisible losses. There might be the loss of freedom and of independence, saying farewell to old roles, cherished dreams, excitement and involvement. We can feel 'let down'. This 'let-down' factor can follow hard on the absolute joy and relief and satisfaction of having achieved our goals. Complicating this 'let down' feeling is the intensity of other feelings – our guilt and shame at not being more happy and relieved. We might wonder what is *wrong* with us. Instead of feeling elated, we might feel mildly deflated. We might feel confused and disgruntled. However, at a conscious level, we might not make the connection between the apparent success and the 'let down' feeling. In fact, some people become irritated if such a connection is pointed out to them. On the face of things, it doesn't make sense.

These 'let downs' might be referred to as 'success depressions' and they can be relieved by recognising the loss and doing some grief-work at the level that is necessary. The grief-work involved in accepting the loss of freedom which new parenthood brings might be quite different from that involved in adjusting to retirement; both of these will be radically different from the grief-work involved in accepting the loss of a significant person in our lives.

ECHOES OF THE PAST

One loss can remind us of another, previous loss. At times, this reminder is not a conscious one. Nevertheless, a current loss can trigger feelings connected with a past loss. For instance, not getting that much wanted promotion at work might trigger a similar sense of loss you felt when you didn't get into graduate school or make it into the school orchestra.

A female client, a woman in her forties came for counselling, concerned about her reaction to a lover's rejection. As she verbalised her despair,

I began to understand that her sense of loss and feelings of pain were not only related to the loss of this man, but also to previous, equally crushing losses of significant people in her life.

Frances had not made the connection – at least not consciously. But what she told me allowed me to see the connection – and to help her gain insight into the history of losses in her life and the links between them.

Frances had had a difficult relationship with her father, who left the family home when she was 12. She didn't see him again until she was 18. She describes him as a 'distant man' but one she admired for his achievements and strength of character. When she made contact with him at 18, at her instigation, she found him to be much warmer and 'fatherly' than she had remembered. For a year, she enjoyed his company every second week-end and she grew close to him. Ironically, it was when their relationship was at its best point, that she lost him – forever. Her father died in a motor accident and as Frances said, *'I never got the chance to say goodbye'*. So painful was this for Frances, that she spent many years driving her pain inward, not allowing any tears to flow – and becoming sexually promiscuous.

At 30, she settled down and married. Two years later she had a son. Again, not consciously, Frances invested a lot of emotional energy in her son and she became the 'perfect mother'. But several years later, after hearing stories of her husband's infidelity, she decided to have an affair herself. As she tells the story all these years later, she's surprised how 'calculated' her decision had been. At the time, it seemed *'you know, natural – like, well, if he can, so can I'*.

Sitting with her, I sensed she had become aware of some of her psychological processes – she had gained some insight. She had decided to reject her husband, before she, was rejected by him. She flaunted her affair, whereas he had been discreet. She laughed at herself, saying *'it was the old case of the wife hearing rumours and being the last to find out'*.

But her unresolved grief over her father's death had made her vulnerable. She wasn't going to be rejected by another man. Frances had made sure her marriage was in jeopardy. After her separation and divorce, Frances said she lived life to the full. Then she met her lover and settled down. She dreamed of a blissful relationship with him. He was sensitive and warm and they shared many interests. So how could he leave her after five years? Frances was disbelieving at first. Then she was mad. Finally, she was distraught.

She sobbed and sobbed. She looked up at me and said, *'Life isn't fair. Brendan left me. My husband left me. My father left me. And my son will leave me soon. Why does everyone leave me? I think I'll have to give up relationships with men. I can't suffer another loss'.*

Yes, Frances, you're right – life isn't fair. I acknowledged her pain and her sense of loss. I asked her how she saw herself responding to these losses.

She said she didn't know. Ah-ha. Maybe that was the problem. Frances had a revelation. Maybe she had never grieved at each loss point. Just maybe her losses were mounting in their enormity after each experience – because unfinished business was carried forward. The cumulative effects of unfinished business can be very traumatic. She had said it. Brendan had left her, her husband had left her and before him, her father had left her. Each loss was experienced, but her feelings had been left unfinished. What's more, Frances is right. In the future, her son will leave her. How will she cope with that if she hasn't grieved for her previous losses?

Frances and I decided we should work towards Frances resolving her sense of loss – in retrospect – and each loss was to be laid to rest. That way, new losses would not trigger old loss feelings. At the very least, she could feel more confident in dealing with any future losses, knowing she has been able to resolve past ones.

Over the next few sessions, Frances moved from feeling like she got all the bad breaks to resolving not to feel and behave like a 'good-bye girl'. She laughed as she recalled the humour of ***The Good-bye Girl***, the film starring Richard Dreyfus and Marsha Mason. It told the story of a young woman, who came to believe that her life was a string of relationship loss – and that she would remain the 'good-bye girl' to men forever more. This sort of unresolved grief can happen, when a person, for whatever reasons, has not done their 'good grief' work.

Making our losses conscious and making connections between our losses is the start of a process which helps us move to a point where we are not scared of facing new losses. That's the process that Frances embarked on. And it helped her change her image of herself as a woman who is always rejected by the important men in her life.

Looking at the history of our life losses can help us understand what we've been through – and remind us of how we have coped – and will cope again.

Making connections between the loss, your views about that loss – and the decision you made at the time – and your present predicament may move you towards a more sound resolution.

Remember, if you don't deal with the thoughts and feelings around your life loss – your issues around grieving remain unresolved. Simply saying, 'I'll deal with it when I feel stronger', or 'I'll look at all this some day' is not enough. Unresolved loss – and unresolved grief – stay with us and affect our coping style, in the present and into the future.

A good way to look at your losses and to ponder which losses you have dealt with and which might still be unresolved is by drawing a life-line of life losses.

Exercise   A life-line of life losses

This exercise can be very powerful. You might have an intensely emotional experience in doing this task. Try to stay with your thoughts and feelings – and write them out at the end.

Directions

Sit in a comfortable position. Clear your mind of the immediate thoughts you have. Concentrate on your task of looking at your life-line and marking your life losses.

Take a clean piece of paper – or a new leaf in your journal and draw a horizontal line across the paper. Put a dot at each end of the line. The left hand dot represents your birth date – write this under the dot. The right hand line represents the current date – write this also under the dot.

Look carefully at this line. Study it. Now, mark with a vertical line each five-year period of your life. Let this chronology settle into your consciousness.
When you are ready, chart your life losses chronologically along the five-year bands.

A sample chart might look like this:

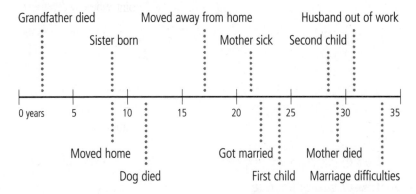

| | | | | | | | | |

Exercise **Writing out your thoughts and feelings**

When you have drawn your chart, take a good look. When was your first life loss? What was this first loss? Are there any periods where more than one loss occurred around the same time?

Now, you might like to add to your chronological chart, the decisions you made and the changes that occurred in your life as a result of a particular loss.

This life-line graph – your chronology of life losses gives you the opportunity of understanding your loss history and how you have coped. And how you might be affected by a current – or a possible loss. Have any of these losses been unresolved? If so, take your pen and write whatever comes into your mind about your thoughts and feelings about that loss.

Recall one key loss in your life narrative.
Is there anything else you'd like to write about regarding your losses?
Look back over what you have written. Are you surprised by anything? If so, what?
Now, put your writing aside. Leave it for a few days, maybe even a week.
Then take it out and look at it afresh.

You might learn something else about how you cope with your life losses by coming back to your chart and your writings after putting them aside. Sometimes, we develop different ways of seeing things after we've had a chance to process them in our minds. Maybe you'll be surprised by some discoveries about yourself.

Remember, learning to understand yourself and your coping style is the first step in your recovery. It is the first step in learning to cope with life after loss.

TYPES OF LOSSES

It is important to familiarise ourselves with losses – small and large, minor and major. Paying attention to smaller losses might help us to better understand loss as part of our daily life. By reflecting on the way smaller losses affect our lives, we can partially prepare for the inevitable major losses we all experience.

Losses can be grouped into categories. One such categorisation of losses is divided into five parts:

1. **Loss of a significant person** (through death, separation or divorce)

2. **Loss of part of the self**:
   (a) physical loss (loss or damage to part of the body or to body functions)
   (b) psychological loss (loss of self-esteem, status, ideals, hopes, control, independence, choice)
   (c) social loss (moving home, loss of employment)
   (d) cultural loss (social network changes, spiritual changes, migration)

3. **Loss of possessions** (personal items such as property, jewellery, money)

4. **Developmental loss** (adolescence, starting school, leaving school, marriage, middle age, old age)

5. **Loss of freedom** (loss of mobility, sense of confinement, imprisonment)

Adapted from Simons

Looking at this category of losses and changes, you might think that some are temporary losses and changes. However, a person's response to even a temporary loss can be complicated. For example, if your car is stolen and subsequently, you get it back, the loss is not permanent. Nevertheless, at the time, it would feel permanent. Not only that, some people have reported that they view their car differently, less positively, because of its temporary loss.

In one sense, the fifth category, 'loss of freedom' is closely related to the second category in that there is a loss of part of the self at various levels, for instance, psychological loss, social loss and cultural loss.

Exercise   Categorising your losses

Look at your life line from the previous exercise. Examine your life line and determine into which of the following categories your examples fit. For instance, your losses may be mainly related to loss of significant people, or you may have experienced psychological losses along with developmental losses as well.

Categories of losses

Loss of significant person	Loss of external object	Developmental loss	Loss of part of the self			
			Physical	Social	Psychological	Community
Mother	Money	Birth	Illness	Status	Trauma	Religion
Father	House	Childhood	Stroke	Roles	Memory	Culture
Sister	Photos	Starting school	Arthritis	House	Control	
Brother	Jewellery	Leaving school	Infertility	Infertility	Esteem	
Baby or child	Property	Adulthood	Amputation		Pride	
Grandparents	Personal possessions	Marriage	Blindness		Ideals	
Uncle	Pets	Divorce	Deafness		Freedom	
Aunt			Menopause		Independence	
Friend		Retirement			Status or job	
		Old age				

Adapted from McBride, 1996

Remember, losses may overlap one or more categories. For instance, loss of employment would fit the category 'loss of external object' but may also mean loss of social status (loss of part of self: social) and loss of pride (loss of part of self: psychological).

Remember also, that some experiences of loss comprise events that everyone experiences. For example, those developmental losses involved in moving from childhood to adolescence and then to adulthood. However, there are also unique experiences. For instance, not everyone experiences failure to be admitted to a much wanted educational course, or a bankruptcy.

Sometimes, people may not associate some events with a loss, or at least, not appreciate the potential for an event to symbolise a loss. For instance, women who have experienced rape often talk about the loss of control, of loss of trust, loss of self-worth and sometimes loss of innocence, all of which are psychological losses.

After completing this exercise, take five minutes to reflect on what you have learnt. Write down three things you have learnt.

WRITING THROUGH YOUR LOSS AND GRIEF

Writing is a powerful form of expression for grieving people. It is a form of therapy, which can be done any time of the day or night. You can choose when to write and when you won't. Some people have called journals 'the paper psychiatrists'.

Rabbi Earl A. Grollman in his book, **When Someone You Love Has Alzheimer's**, says of journal writing: *'A journal is a place where you can say anything you wish without being pitied, judged, criticized, or made uncomfortable. There is a difference between writing your thought and speaking them out loud in public. 'Journaling' helps you to express your feelings, especially when you feel isolated and find it difficult to communicate with others.'*

You are invited to use writing as a way of healing.

You can write by hand, in a notebook or a journal with a favourite pen. Or you can write on a typewriter or computer – but it's important for you to print out what you write, so that you can touch it, see it and read it.

Remember, that writing can bring to the surface painful emotions and memories. It can be part of your grief-work to recognise that this is happening and to pay attention to such feelings. It is important that you assess how much you can face your feelings at any point in time. However, it is equally important for you to be aware that denying your feelings, distracting yourself and busying yourself with activities might act to push your feelings down. In the long-term, such unresolved feelings not faced and dealt with may compound, resurface and delay your grief-work.

Keeping a journal of your thoughts and feelings might work for you. **'Prompts for your pen'** exercises throughout these pages will help you record and work on your loss and grief.

Writing, in a journal:

- is a way to explore and gain understanding of your emotions
- clarifies thought
- records information
- allows expression of feeling
- is a non-judgmental friend
- provides a place to escape from reality for a while
- can be done anyplace, anytime
- assists the writer to come to terms with things
- fosters creativity
- puts loss into a tangible perspective
- is a safe venue for processing fear, anger, guilt and other emotions you can explore.

SOME VIEWS ON WRITING AS HEALING

Many famous writers have openly written or implied that: writing helped them heal, writing changed their lives or that writing itself, saved their lives. Celebrated writers who found writing healing include: Sylvia Plath, Anne Sexton, Anais Nin, Isabel Allende, Simone de Beauvoir, Jamaica Kincaid, May Sarton, Anne Morrow Linbergh, Alice Walker, Virginia Woolf, Toni Morrison, James Baldwin, Henry Miller, D. H. Lawrence, C. S. Lewis.

Ray Bradbury, writing in ***Zen in the Art of Writing***, said:

'So while our art cannot, as we wish it could, save us from wars, privation, envy, greed, old age, or death, it can revitalize us amidst it all...
Writing is survival...
Not to write, for many of us, is to die.'

Jamaica Kincaid's view is similar to Ray Bradbury's and expressed in the following lines:

'I became a writer out of desperation... When I was young, younger than I am now, I started to write about my own life and I came to see that this act saved my life.'

Simone de Beauvoir chronicled her mother's illness and death and her reactions to the experience in *A Very Easy Death*. Simone de Beauvoir was surprised that she needed to write through her experience, because she did not expect her mother's death to *'shake me so deeply'*. She begins the book by marking the day that she heard of her mother's accident. She was in Rome when she heard that her mother had sustained a fracture, which was the beginning of investigations that led to a diagnosis of cancer. It is interesting that Simone de Beauvoir, like many others, recalls the day, date and time of hearing the news. She writes:

> *'At four o'clock in the afternoon of Thursday, 24 October 1963, I was in Rome, in my room at the Hotel Minerva; I was to fly home the next day and I was putting papers away when the telephone rang.'*

In telling their stories, grieving people often begin by informing the listener of these exact details. The details are a marker and almost indelibly imprinted on people's memories. It's the beginning of the story.

Mark Doty offers writing as healing to help us come to terms with our challenges. He wrote in *Heaven's Coast*: *'What is healing, but a shift in perspective?'*

By keeping a journal and writing, you may find your necessary shift in perspective.

The healing shifts for Virginia Woolf came from her writing about psychic wounds. She believed that our moments of profound insight come from writing about our soulful and honest examination of our psychic wounds – and these should be called 'shocks'. These 'shocks' act to force us into a greater awareness of ourselves and our relationship to others and our place in the world.

Alice Walker, author of *The Color Purple*, remarked that writing, not only for her, but for us all, can be *'a matter of necessity and that you write to save your life is really true and so far it's been a very sturdy ladder out of the pit.'*

In Isabel Allende's *Paula*, a memoir about her daughter's terminal illness and death, she describes how she began writing her famous novel, *House of the Spirits*. Originally, it was meant to be a farewell letter to her elderly grandfather, whom she was unable to visit. Allende was in exile, but she began **House of the Spirits** as *'an anecdote about my great-aunt Rosa, my grandfather's first sweetheart, a young girl of almost supernatural beauty who had died in mysterious circumstances shortly before they were to marry.'*

Allende continued to write as if in a trance – she felt she was *'unwinding a ball of yarn'*. In fact, her personal letter to her grandfather grew into a 500 page manuscript. Allende says that writing **House of the Spirits** *'saved my life'*. She began the book as a form of self-care, to express her grief and through writing she said, *'the world became more tolerable. Living with myself was more tolerable too.'*

Allende recalls how her literary agent, Carmen Balcells encouraged her to write of her pain and desperation after her daughter, Paula, lapsed into a coma. Carmen deposited *'a ream of lined yellow paper'* into Allende's lap.

"My poor Isabel," Balcells said. *"Here, take this and write. Unburden your heart; if you don't you are going to die of anguish."*

Allende protested that something inside her had 'broken' and she believed she would never write again. However, Balcells commanded Allende to *'write a letter to Paula. It will help her know what happened while she was asleep.'* Balcells encouraged Allende to write, knowing that without the release of words, Allende's health would suffer. Balcells feared that Allende might succumb to a serious illness in the wake of her daughter's condition and Allende's grief.

Allende wrote to her comatose daughter, *'I plunge into these pages in an irrational attempt to overcome my terror. I think that perhaps if I give form to this devastation I shall be able to help you, and myself, and that the meticulous exercise of writing can be our salvation.'*

For writing to be a healing experience, we need to honour our loss, pain and grief. We need to witness our thoughts and feelings instead of denying them or ignoring them. By doing this work, we are likely to experience a shift in our perspective, as Mark Doty suggests.

Your writing can take any form you wish. Keeping a journal, writing stories or poems are all ways of getting in touch with your feelings and your grief.

PROMPTS FOR YOU PEN

| Exercise | Reflections on your healing through writing |

- You can begin with a letter like Isabel Allende did.
  Can you transform it into a poem or story?

- Read D. H. Lawrence's poem 'Piano'

> *Softly, in the dusk, a woman is singing to me;*
>
> *Taking me back down the vista of year, till I see*
>
> *A child sitting under the piano, in the boom of the tingling strings*
>
> *And pressing the small poised feet of a mother who smiles as she sings.*
>
> *In spite of myself, the insidious master of song*
>
> *Betrays me back, till the heart of me weeps to belong*
>
> *To the old Sunday evenings at home, with winter outside*
>
> *And hymns in the cosy parlour, the tinkling piano our guide.*
>
> *So now it is vain for the singer to burst into clamour*
>
> *With the great black piano appassionato. The glamour*
>
> *Of childish days is upon me, my manhood is cast*
>
> *Down in the flood of remembrance, I weep like a child for the past.*

- Reflect on D. H. Lawrence's poem. What does it mean to you?
  Can you relate to the sadness and nostalgia by reflecting on your own past?
  What memories does it stir for you?

- Are there any losses in your life you feel compelled to write about?

Why not keep a daily journal?
Perhaps you might consider keeping a journal of your journey through grief.

PROMPTS FOR YOU PEN

Exercise	Keeping a daily journal of my journey

Each day, record the following information:

• date and time of your entry at the top of each page
• a significant happening of the day
• a person who was most important to you today
• changes you observe happening to you
• your plans for tomorrow
• notes for yourself

People have reported that they find it helpful to write their journal at about the same time every day. Perhaps you might develop this habit and then your journaling will become second nature.

The importance of a daily journal will become clear weeks, months or maybe even years down the track. At times, you might feel you are making no progress, but by reading back through your journal, you will be reminded where you have been and how far you have come.

One important value of the journal is that it helps you to stay in charge of your grief experience. It provides a measure of guidance through the chaos of the experience and it helps you internalise the insights you have gained in your writing.

2

THE BROKEN HEART: UNDERSTANDING GOOD GRIEF

Life must go on;
I forget just why.

EDNA ST. VINCENT MILLAY [Lament]

In our future-oriented, scientific society, older wisdoms often are regarded as obsolete, as mere superstitions. Folk wisdom over the centuries told of an association between loss of a loved one and illness. A century ago, people would talk about dying of a 'broken heart'. Today, such expressions are used only metaphorically. Yet, research findings highlight the validity of the notion that a grieving person is a 'person at risk'. Studies have found that widows and widowers are in a category where the rate of illness or mortality is very high.

In 1961, the English psychiatrist George Engel compared loss with a physical wound. He pointed out that in both cases, the wound has to heal up. Dr Engel spoke about grief-work as the healthy process which slowly heals the wounds of the psyche. Much as a physical wound will fester if regenerating forces do not act as they should, so too with the psychic wound. If the healing forces of grief are out of action, the wound will not heal.

Dr Engel asked 'Is grief a disease?' We might respond by saying no, grief is not a disease. However, it can develop into one. It might be possible to die of a 'broken heart'.

The yesteryear concept of dying of a 'broken heart' was updated by Dr Colin Murray Parkes and associates in a study of 4,500 British widowers, 55 years of age and older.

They found that the death rate during the first six months of grieving was 40% higher than that expected for married men the same age. Later in the grieving period, the rates for the widowers gradually fell to the married level. Interestingly, the greatest increase in mortality was in those who died from heart disease – the 'broken heart' idea of antiquity.

Later investigations similarly have shown that people in grief are both physically and mentally or psychically, under greater threat than others.

Dr James J. Lynch, a specialist in psychosomatic medicine wrote in **_The Broken Heart: the Medical Consequences of Loneliness_**:

'A few hundred years ago 'grief' was openly recognized as a cause of death. Today, however, a broken heart would never be listed as a cause of death in any U.S. hospital. We have grown far too 'medically wise' to tolerate such an ill-defined diagnosis... Despite modern medical science's reluctance to recognize the killing potential of human grief, most physicians are intuitively aware of its lethal power. While most physicians would never list 'grief' or 'loneliness' or a 'broken heart' as a cause of death, that does not mean they do not recognize the importance of these emotional factors in heart disease.'

It is possible to reconcile old and new ways of thinking. With out modern ways of understanding stress, we might have an explanation of how grief and illness are linked. The belief that 'grief will make you sick' is a folk saying that over a half a century ago, Dr Walter B. Cannon was exploring. As a physiologist and pioneer in the role of emotions in bodily functioning, he believed that stress had a major role in creating illness. More recent findings have reported connections between asthma, ulcerative colitis, rheumatoid arthritis, a variety of heart diseases and hypertension – and grief. It is not understood clearly why grief should show itself in certain people in particular diseases, however, the suggestion has been made that stress is inextricably part of the picture.

In grief – the sense of loss and the challenges of meeting unwelcome changes – does produce stress. By understanding the possible physical and emotional aspects of grief, people will be able to protect themselves from additional stresses and illnesses. If a person avoids the pain and torment – and the feeling of mastery in overcoming the grief – then he or she might pay dearly for this avoidance in inadequate or uncompleted grief.

Experiencing 'good grief' and doing 'grief-work' is important. Inadequate attention to working through grief might lead to further stresses and illness – the wound may fester. The unfinished business of grief can lead to a grieving that never ends.

Remember: There are no fixed or prescribed ways of reacting to loss. People react to losses in very different ways. But there is always anguish and pain associated with loss. In fact, for some people, the pain can be so great that they turn to drugs or alcohol, in search of a solution through chemical comforts. While these chemical aids may be helpful and consoling in the short-term, they have the potential to create further problems.

While we are unique, some responses to losses are similar. It is generally agreed that death is the most significant loss. Death is final. And it reminds us of our mortality. However, our pain at losing a much cherished dream, being fired from work or being jilted can make us feel sad and down and we hurt. We are in pain.

Pain can begin with a confusing variety of emotions. Unanswerable questions become part of life.

Your loss may trigger any or all of the following states and emotions:

- Disbelief
- Shock
- Anger
- Confusion
- Loss of interests
- Guilt
- Insomnia
- Panic

- Anxiety
- Resentment
- Fear of losing control
- Bargaining
- Crying and sobbing
- Yearning and pining
- Depression
- Disorganisation

- Denial
- Helplessness
- Loneliness
- Lowered self-esteem

The depth and duration of any of these states or emotions is very much an individual matter. Living with them is part of the process of coming to terms with them.

We must recognise the importance of our loss. Expressing our feelings and telling the story of our loss help us to understand the grief process. It is our task in the face of loss to find effective ways to cope. We need to get over the emotional pains and we need to let them go. Only by coping and letting go can be grow from this painful experience.

William Shakespeare recognised the importance of telling our story, when he wrote:

'Give sorrow words: the grief that does not speak
Whispers the o-er-fraught heart, and bids it break.

Macbeth, Act V, Scene 1

This 'giving sorrow words' can be done verbally, in writing or in some other artistic manner.

Recovering from the pain – and understanding the loss and grief in the context of our unique world is essential if we are to heal the inner and outer wounds of our life – and to mend and heal our hearts.

Sometimes, people cling to their pain because they don't know how to let it go. They have never learned. Maybe they haven't had role models to follow, or perhaps they have never been challenged before to think about the philosophy and assumptions of their daily life. However, by clinging to grief and pain, people may believe they are protecting themselves from further pain.

This is a deception. By clinging to the wreckage, so to speak, people are protecting themselves also from living fully and growing through the experience.

Remember: We have to recognise that new losses also may reactivate old, unresolved losses and grief.

Ruth, an elderly Jewish woman told me that the death of her granddaughter reactivated her old grief of losing her family in a death camp. She relived the pain with her young granddaughter's accidental death. It was at this point that she realised that she had never truly resolved her feelings of loss around being deprived of most of her family. Her loss stretched back half a century and into the future. With the loss of her granddaughter, she relived the pain of losing another generation. For Ruth, too many generations had been lost. Part of her future had been lost – along with a lot of her past.

Ruth was fond of writing poetry. In the past, she had avoided personally painful themes. She had turned her attention to and written about the 'bigger picture', about her concern for the environment and the plight of humanity in an ever more alienating and impersonal world. Although it was difficult for her, she decided to write poems to resolve all her past losses. She said she had never 'had the courage' to put her feelings down on paper before. She had secretly believed she would 'lose' her mind if she did – it would be too traumatic. She had been frightened of seeing the power of her emotions. Several months later, Ruth showed her poems to me and I was touched. It had been a big step for her to write about her losses, which she had kept locked away. Now she had written about these huge losses and faced them on paper. To her surprise, it had been a healing exercise. Painful, yes. But also healing. She shared the overwhelming emotions she'd felt after writing her poems. Her anger, despair, guilt about surviving and helplessness in the face of life's cruel lessons were put down on paper. Ruth spoke about a 'release' and 'a new understanding' of her emotions and her life. This release and understanding came after a week of feelings of helplessness, guilt and weeping. Ruth had not wept for years, believing it was a sign of being out of control. She told me she had learned a valuable lesson in irony,

'you have to let yourself get out of control to find the control inside you'.
As in the story of **The first tear**, weeping eased Ruth's pain, and indeed
became a 'precious treasure' which allowed her to find new strength.

Ruth's story highlights how a loss occurring at an earlier stage in your life
can have a huge effect on later life. Having to deal with intense feelings of
sadness, guilt, rage, abandonment, anxiety – or any of many other states and
feelings – is an enormous challenge. Often we can't meet the entire challenge.
So the original challenge may be magnified when the next loss is faced.

REACTIONS TO LOSS

Loss, then, is universal. And we all have similar reactions. If only fleetingly.
For some people, these reactions linger, and perhaps even hinder their ability
to deal appropriately with their loss.

- We feel as if we are alone. Perhaps nobody really understands.
- We feel like our lives are breaking into small, useless fragments.
- We believe that loss has broken our hearts and damaged our souls.
- We feel broken, perhaps beyond repair – mending and healing our hearts
  seems too big a task.

Of course, on an intellectual level, we know that millions of other people
have experienced loss similar to ours. However, on an emotional level, we
feel that no-one else in the world has ever felt as crushed as we do. We are
certain that no-one could possibly have felt the same tearing pain, intense
agony and immense sadness which haunts us. We believe no-one else could
ever have experienced the same level of loneliness, the same emptiness
which fills seemingly every waking moment and often creeps into our
dreams. We believe no-one really understands what we're going through.

You might ask yourself: 'Why is there no-one who understands me?'
You wish desperately that someone did. The truth is that many of us do
understand.

Response to loss is a very individual matter, and yet, there are universal
aspects to all our losses. That's because of the similarities that exist within all
loss. Because all losses have in them threads of similarity, anyone who has

been on the emotional roller-coaster of one can relate to the inner torment which is part of another. All losses, to varying degrees, create within us pain, fear, sorrow, anger, guilt and confusion. All loss temporarily frustrates us and immobilises us. All loss isolates us, for a time, from the mainstream of life.

Our losses can make us feel very inadequate. Marina told me how she felt. She said, *'After my mastectomy, I felt like I was not whole. I was in fragments. I felt so inadequate because I was not coping. I wasn't accepting myself. I felt alone. And I felt that no-one out there really could understand how a woman of 34 feels when she loses her left breast.'*

Through her attendance at a support group, Marina slowly came to understand she was not alone. She also found that other women – both older and younger – did understand the sense of trauma and grief a woman feels when she loses a breast.

Our losses can also make us feel vulnerable. Jackie had lost her toddler in a swimming pool drowning. Her guilt was enormous. Her sense of loss gigantic. She says, *'I wanted to just howl. I mean just sit and howl until I was hoarse. But I couldn't. I couldn't be seen to be losing my sanity. I think keeping it in made me more vulnerable. You know, the damage was greater. Someone told me that in Zaire people can sit and howl for days on end. And they say that people heal so much quicker. As it was, it wasn't until I joined a support group and heard others talking that I felt I could say all the crazy things I felt. It helps to know what you're feeling is normal.'*

CRYING, WEEPING AND HOWLING

This idea that Jackie has about the possible benefits of what she calls 'howling' has been found to be the case in studies and clinical observations of clients who have suffered loss and feel grief.

As the old Jewish story at the beginning of this chapter highlighted, the tear is symbolic of the most precious treasure, a costly pearl, because *'when someone is in pain and feels great grief, tears flow from his eyes. And behold! The grief eases.'*

Alexander Lowen, the founder of bioenergetics, has this to say about weeping:

'Weeping, accompanied by sobbing is the first and and deepest release of tensions. Children can weep without trouble in connection with all stress influences that produce a state of tension in the body. First, the child's body is tensed, then its jaw trembles, and immediately afterwards it breaks out in a convulsion-like release of tension. Man (sic) is the only animal that can react to stress and tensions in this way.'

As we grow and develop as humans, we lose this inherent ability of the child to reduce stress through tears. And, often parents, embarrassed or anxious by the crying of their children, will tell them, 'It's nothing to cry about'. This message of 'learn to control yourself' is one that many children hear in childhood. And the consequence is that such a message may ultimately impair the child's – and the adult's capacity to grieve. Crying might well be a wholesome and natural way to express distress and resolve stress – both bodily and psychologically.

Shedding tears is very difficult for some people. Yet, the old Jewish story might well hold the key. For the 'most precious treasure', the tear might well help to restore the body's natural balance in the face of stress. Recent studies have suggested that the chemical content of tears shed in distress – weeping tears – are different from normal 'watering' or 'teary' eyes. These tears of sadness release substances that have a calming effect. So, it's no myth that having a good cry makes you feel better.

Sylvia Plath wrote movingly about unresolved grief, reawakened grief and weeping. The following excerpt, from **The Bell Jar** also demonstrates her use of writing as healing.

'I tugged my black veil down to my chin and strode in through the wrought-iron gates. I thought it odd that in all the time my father had been buried in this graveyard, none of us had ever visited him. My mother hadn't let us come to his funeral because we were only children then, and he had died in the hospital, so the graveyard and even his death had always seemed unreal to me.

I had a great yearning, lately, to pay my father back for the years of neglect, and start tending his grave. I had always been my father's favorite, and it seemed fitting I should take on a mourning my mother had never bothered with.

I thought that if my father hadn't died, he would have taught me all about insects, which was his specialty at the university. He would also have taught me German and Greek and Latin, which he knew, and perhaps I would be a Lutheran. My father had been a Lutheran in Wisconsin, but they were out of style in New England, so he had become a lapsed Lutheran and then, my mother said, a bitter atheist.

The graveyard disappointed me. It lay at the outskirts of the town, on low ground, like a rubbish dump, and as I walked up and down the gravel paths, I could smell the stagnant salt marshes in the distance.

The old part of the graveyard was all right, with its worn flat stones and lichen-bitten monuments, but I soon saw my father must be buried in the modern part with dates in the nineteen forties.

The stones in the modern part were crude and cheap, and here and there a grave was rimmed with marble, like an oblong bathtub full of dirt, and rusty metal containers stuck up about where the person's navel would be, full of plastic flowers.

A fine drizzle started drifting down from the gray sky, and I grew very depressed.

I couldn't find my father anywhere.

Low, shaggy clouds scudded over that part of the horizon where the sea lay, behind the marshes and the beach shanty settlements, and raindrops darkened the black mackintosh I had bought that morning. A clammy dampness sank through to my skin.

I had asked the salesgirl, 'Is it water-repellent?'

And she had said, 'No raincoat is ever water-repellent. It's showerproofed.'

And when I asked her what showerproofed was, she told me I had better buy an umbrella.

But I hadn't enough money for an umbrella. What with the bus fare in and out of Boston and peanuts and newspapers and abnormal-psychology books and trips to my old home town by the sea, my New York fund was almost exhausted.

I had decided that when there was no more money in my bank account I would do it, and that morning I'd spend the last of it on the black raincoat.

Then I saw my father's gravestone.

It was crowded right up by another gravestone, head to head, the way people are crowded in a charity ward when there isn't enough space. The stone was of a mottled pink marble, like canned salmon, and all there was on it was my father's name and, under it, two dates, separated by a little dash.

At the foot of the stone I arranged the rainy armful of azaleas I had picked from a bush at the gateway of the graveyard. Then my legs folded under me, and I sat down on the sopping grass. I couldn't understand why I was crying so hard.

Then I remembered that I had never cried for my father's death.

My mother hadn't cried either. She had just smiled and said what a merciful thing it was for him he had died, because if he had lived he would have been crippled and an invalid for life, and he couldn't have stood that, he would rather have died than had that happen.

I laid my face to the smooth face of the marble and howled my loss into the cold salt rain.'

PROMPT FOR YOUR PEN

Exercise	Questions for reflection

- What are the main themes in Sylvia Plath's account?
- Can you identify with aspects of her experience?
- What do you make of her crying and howling?

Weeping may make some people feel vulnerable, yet, it could also be something which could begin their healing process. Vulnerability expressed can result in strength. It is the irony of life, that perhaps only by making ourselves vulnerable – and facing our demons – can we be strengthened ultimately.

On the journey to good grief, you might shed more tears than you thought your body could hold. One widow commented that she had cried enough to fill an Olympic-size swimming pool – and added, *'No wonder they say the body is mostly made up of water!'*

In this sense, our losses, can also strengthen us. In the words of the poet William Blake:

He who bends to himself a joy
Does the winged life destroy;
But he who kisses the Joy as it flies
Lives in eternity's sunrise.

Betty Jane Wylie, writing movingly about the sudden death of her 45-year-old husband has made some valuable observations about the grieving process, and the need to be vulnerable in order to make ourselves stronger. She says,

'Speed is not necessarily a good thing. Well-meaning friends are anxious to get everything done, arranged, finished, so that you can start getting over it. You don't ever get over it. Loss is permanent. Part of you has died, too. So a little wallowing at this time doesn't hurt, if people would only allow it. But our society seems to demand that we behave ourselves at funerals, and after. And we usually do. Deportment is all. Breakdowns are bad form. But a little howling at the moon might save a lot of tension later on.'

There it is again. That theme of crying – or as Betty Jane Wylie calls it 'a little howling at the moon' can release stresses and tensions.

Dealing with our loss can be liberating and empowering. It can make us stronger. Janis tells her story of loss faced and grief resolved. At the age of 8, the literal loss of her younger sister and the perceived loss of her mother had plunged her into years of confusion and unhappiness. After her sister's death from childhood leukemia, her mother seemingly withdrew from family life. Janis believed her mother had abdicated her responsibility as 'my mum'. Fortunately for Janis, she had a sensitive father who took over where his wife had left off. Janis also had her mother's sister, a woman who was unable to have children – and who became Janis's surrogate mother. Twenty-five years later, Janis can see how her early loss had strengthened her for the ups and downs of her future life.

From her present vantage point, Janis can see how people around her helped her resolve her losses and get on with her life, strengthened for the experience. She said,

> 'My father was the sort of man who was interested in feelings, in matters of the heart. I think he went out of his way to make sure my mother's rejection of me, of me and him, wasn't going to damage me. He made up for her emotional absence. He allowed me to express myself. He brought my aunt into the picture and let her take a big role in my life. He wasn't threatened by her. I believe he knew it was important for me to have a functioning and positive female role-model – and my aunt Marianne was that. She was warm and loving. She also helped me express my disappointment at having lost my mum. Both she and my dad were accepting human beings and they showed me by example and encouragement that I could mourn the loss of my mother's love – and celebrate the warmth of their acceptance and unconditional love.'

Janis goes on to comment that her early positive experience of losing but resolving and getting on with life has meant that she fears loss less intensely than she might otherwise do. In fact, she commented that many of her friends don't appear to 'believe in themselves' and she's seen some of them 'fall apart' in the face of experiences of loss. She adds that she's always 'there' for her friends, because she believes in the old saying that 'sharing is caring'.

Sharing can be healing. In examining Janis's early experience, we can see that her father and aunt were sharing with her their own loss experience and in so doing, they offered her – and themselves – healing.

GRIEF: THE IRRETRIEVABLE LOSS OF THE FAMILIAR

What is grief? Any number of definitions can be given here. How do we use the word 'grief' in everyday language? Will that give us a clue?

'She has a heavy heart. Her husband of forty years died. She is grieving.'
(She is sad and lonely, lost and helpless, because her husband has died)

'That child will come to grief if he rides his bike that way.'
(He will fall off his bike the way he is going)

'She will come to grief, if she's not careful'.
(She'll be in trouble if she doesn't watch out)

'My client has a grievance'
(The client has briefed an attorney to take legal proceedings regarding some wrong done to him)

'It grieves me to tell you that your application has not been successful'
(It hurts me to give you the following news)

'Good grief!'
(an exclamation of surprise or alarm, used colloquially)

All these sentences use the words 'grief' in some specific way. Over the centuries, the word has become associated with several similar, yet slightly different meanings. From the fear that a child may come to grief on his bike to the legalistic meaning of bringing a complaint before the court, the word 'grief' encapsulates the idea of a cause or consequence of grieving. The word's most common usage, however, is related to the idea of loss and grief. In everyday conversation we consciously recognise the meaning of the words 'grief' and 'grieving' as pertaining to unhappiness and trauma.

Grief then, is a reaction to any significant experience of loss. Retirement is a serious loss. Unfulfilled dreams and hopes are a loss experience. Moving house is a loss of friends and familiar environment. Leaving school or graduation from school may be experienced as difficult losses. Divorce is a loss often said to be worse than death, because the partner goes on living, whereas death is final. Imprisonment is an obvious loss of freedom.

Weddings may symbolise a less obvious loss situation. Entering a nursing home means a loss of independence. Even weaning is a time of loss - for both mother and child.

And because losses are varied and many and because we are all unique, each grief experience is highly personal. Even if a loss is shared, two people will probably grieve differently. A mother might mourn the loss of her son by becoming anxious and withdrawn. Her husband, as the son's father, might become angry and resentful. Or, maybe their responses are the reverse.

It is a mistake to think that we can predict how others will feel and react. C. S. Lewis, in *A Grief Observed* came to the conclusion that there is no template for grief. We must all do our own unique grief-work. He began writing his thoughts and feelings in notebooks. In his words,

> *'In so far as this record was a defence against total collapse, a safety-valve, it has done some good. The other end I had in view turns out to have been based on a misunderstanding. I thought I could describe a state; make a map of sorrow. Sorrow, however, turns out to be not a state but a process. It needs not a map but a history, and if I don't stop writing that history at some quite arbitrary point, there's no reason why I should ever stop. There is something new to be chronicled every day. Grief is like a long valley, a winding valley where any bed may reveal a totally new landscape. As I've already noted, not every bend does. Sometimes the surprise is the opposite one; you are presented with exactly the same sort of country you thought you had left behind miles ago. That is when you wonder whether the valley isn't a circular trench. But it isn't. There are partial recurrences, but the sequence doesn't repeat.'*

The patterns and time of grief, as C. S. Lewis notes are not altogether predictable. Grief does not have a precise timetable, nor does it follow an exact pattern. It is an ongoing process. It is impossible, and dangerous to say that grief will take so many weeks to heal and after that definitive time, the psychic cast can be removed. It is more than a simple disorder in which an X-ray can be taken to show that healing has taken place and it is safe for the person to resume life as they knew it before.

Instead, it is useful to take C. S. Lewis's account and reflect upon the process which healing might take. Gradual change and growth in the grieving person might mean fits and starts, episodes in which issues might recur and new landscapes might appear in the final stages of resolution.

It is reassuring to know that grieving is not a linear process. Grieving is circular and repetitive. We might take 'two steps forwards and one step backwards'. We make progress, more forward and then we retrace our steps. Grieving is not so much continuous as it is recurring. Reminders or past events like holidays and anniversaries and new losses might trigger our grief. One thing is certain, the experience means we are never quite the same again.

Examining how grief feels can prove to be confronting. Often our reactions remind us of other experiences and emotional states. In his notebook, C. S. Lewis wrote movingly and at times chillingly about the feelings involved in the process of grieving. He begins his account with the following startling paragraph: *'No one ever told me that grief felt so like fear. I am not afraid, but the sensation is like being afraid. The same fluttering in the stomach, the same restlessness, the yawning. I keep on swallowing.'*

Indeed, fear can be an overwhelming feeling. Grief can be confusing. Why this feeling of fear? People often talk about how it feels from 'the inside'. From the inside, the grieving person might feel like they are going crazy. It is not uncommon to hear a person say, *'I don't know, sometimes I think I'm going crazy',* or *'Sometimes I feel like I'm losing my mind.'* The changes that inevitably are associated with loss can make us confused, fearful and uncertain.

Most of us resist change. Sometimes, we fear change. However, a loss means change. Change becomes inevitable. We need to face it.

Grief becomes the necessary experience that could well help us survive our loss. Facing our grief and doing 'grief-work' might even mean reaching better self-understanding.

FACT FILE

Freud was the first person to speak about 'the work of mourning'. By this he meant the psychological work that the person who is grieving needs to do to come to terms with what Freud called 'object loss'. This object loss was the loss of something or someone to whom the person was attached. The goal of the grief-work then, is to break the bond between the person grieving (the subject) and the lost person or thing (the object).

Eric Lindemann, the then Chief of Psychiatry at the Massachusetts General Hospital, was the first person to describe the physical and emotional symptoms of acute grief, and he showed that people's reactions are often very similar.

Lindemann shortened Freud's term to 'grief-work'. For him, this meant dealing with the pain of grief, releasing the loss (lost person or lost thing) and readjusting to the subsequent changes in your life. This includes adjusting to the changes in your life and forming a new identity.

In the fall of 1942, two colleges well known for their football rivalry played against one another. Holy Cross beat Boston College. People went to celebrate at the Coconut Grove Nightclub. A decorative palm tree was set on fire when a busboy lit a match whilst changing a lightbulb. The nightclub, which was packed beyond its legal capacity, was enveloped by flames. Five hundred people lost their lives.

Eric Lindemann and his team studied the reactions of those bereaved after this serious fire in which the 500 people died. The familiar patterns they found were the following:

(i) bodily distress of some type
(ii) preoccupation with the image of the lost loved one
(iii) guilt relating to the loved one or the circumstances of their death
(iv) hostile reactions
(v) inability to function as they had before the catastrophic event

Since Lindemann's study, other researchers have found similar phenomena, confirming much of the basis of this work. Some researchers have refined aspects of these patterns.

J. William Worden, Professor of at the Harvard Medical School has devised four categories which comprise a summary of normal grief reactions.

Professor Worden's categories follow:

Feelings (Emotional)

anxiety
fear
sadness
anger
guilt
inadequacy
hurt
relief
loneliness

Cognitions (Mental)

disbelief
confusion
preoccupation
sense of the presence
  of the deceased
hallucinations

Physical (Bodily sensations)

hollowness in the stomach
tightness in the chest
tightness in the throat
over-sensitivity to noise
a sense of depersonalisation
breathlessness
muscle weakness
lack of energy
dry mouth

Behavioural

crying
sleep disturbance
sighing
restlessness and overactivity
appetite disturbances
absentmindedness
social withdrawal
dreams of the deceased
avoiding reminders of the deceased
searching & calling out for the deceased
visiting places and carrying reminders
  of the deceased, or treasuring objects
  which belonged to him or her

Perhaps you've looked at these categories and recognised some of the feelings, thoughts, physical sensations and behaviour as things you've experienced. Maybe you've experienced only some of these things intensely, or maybe you've experienced many of them, some of them more intensely than others. Perhaps some of these feelings and sensations and behaviours were with you briefly, or perhaps they visited with you for much longer. Again, this analysis will turn up the most important point - your individuality. Although studies have informed our understanding, and highlighted typical patterns, your responses are unique to you.

WHAT IS GRIEF-WORK?

Grief-work is the psychological journey a person undertakes to work through their sense of grief. Essentially it has four components:

(i) breaking with the past by recognising the significance of the loss in all its facets

(ii) engaging with the emotions of grief

(iii) rebuilding the present into an adaptable everyday living, incorporating both what is left and some necessary changes

(iv) a recognition of a future with new possibilities and pathways to an adjusted life

Grief-work can be a long and tough process. It is certainly a painful process. Working through confusion, feelings of helplessness and feeling emotionally overwhelmed all takes time – and effort. It also takes the help of others – a supportive social network.

Sometimes people feel like they are going out of their minds. But that may be part of the process.

People should be encouraged to identify and express their emotions - because by doing so, they are less likely to go out of their mind.

Grieving does not proceed in a linear manner. It takes time. And it can often reappear – and then it has to be reworked. How many times have we believed we've resolved a loss only to find that something reawakens it? How many times have we heard others say of the death of a loved one, *'I thought I was over it, but then I was leafing through the photo album and all the pain came back'.*

Remember: The grief experience is individual. There is no point in comparing ourselves to others. Nor is there any point in judging others – we all have our own process to work through. There are so many different factors involved for everyone, that no rules apply. We only have guidelines.

What is known is that grieving involves a process of cutting cords – and that can take time.

UNDERSTANDING YOUR GRIEF

Becoming aware of your unique reaction is important, and it can be difficult. Owning up to all the thoughts, feelings and behaviours associated with grief can be confronting.

Two exercises will follow. Both exercises require you to use your imagination. You might find one easier than the other. The first one asks you to visualise yourself in relation to your loss. Then you make notes of this visualisation for yourself. In the second exercise you are asked to picture your grief – draw it and then add words.

PROMPT FOR YOUR PEN

Exercise **Getting in touch with my own grief**

Step 1: Find yourself a comfortable position and take a few deep breaths. Close your eyes. Focus on your breathing. Slowly clear your mind of any everyday thoughts. Focus on your thoughts around your losses. Visualise the situation for yourself. See yourself, in your mind's eye, responding to these losses.
Now visualise yourself as you are today – where do you stand in relation to your losses? Are you still grieving? Have you resolved your grief?

Step 2: When you are ready, write all your imagery down in words that make sense for you. Try to recapture what you visualised in words.
This is an important record for you.

Don't worry about your spelling or grammar – just get your words down.

You might be surprised at what you felt and wrote down. Sometimes, we can hide, even from ourselves, some of our most innermost thoughts and feelings. We deny them. Not because we are not thinking and feeling beings, but because we are scared of what we really might be thinking and feeling. Our thoughts and feelings are often so powerful that they scare us.

Picturalisation
What does your grief look like?

Exercise — Picturing your grief

Picturing is a powerful tool for you. Creating an image of what grief is like for you might be a first step in understanding its impact on you.

Is grief like a broken heart? Do you think you can mend and heal your heart?

Is your grief like a maze? Do you feel lost and unguided? Is there a safe exit? Do you feel confused by the blind alleys? Do you feel lost and alone?

Is your grief like a jigsaw puzzle? How can you put the pieces back together again to make a whole? Do you know where to begin? Do you sometimes feel you have it coming together, only to find the pieces don't fit anymore?

Is your grief like a stream? Is there safe passage to the other side for you? Are there stepping-stones you can use? Do you feel anxious that you might fall in? Are you frightened that you might be carried away by the rapids?

Which image reminds you of your grief? You might be picturing another image. What is it?

Take a large sheet of paper and some crayons and draw your picturalisation. You don't have to be an artist – just let your thoughts and feelings flow onto the paper.

Sit back when you've finished. Don't rush yourself. Take a good look at your picture. How have you pictured your grief?

Now, it's time to do some free association. Just write down any words which come into your mind.

Think of some words which you could use to explain your picture to someone with whom you might share it.

As a starting point, you can choose some words from the following list – and add to it your own words.

Afraid	Angry	Hurt	Powerless
doubtful	sulky	distressed	numb
quaking	bitter	in pain	in shock
lonely	indignant	suffering	guilty
isolated	resentful	heartbroken	lethargic
restless	worked up	sad	tearful
in a panic	cross	mournful	exhausted
cowardly	irritated	vulnerable	regretful
frightened	offended	crushed	disbelief
threatened	annoyed	tortured	depressed
dismayed	provoked	aching	emptiness

Write these words into your picture wherever you see them as best fitting. You might find they sit around the perimeter of your picture – or perhaps they are written across parts of your image. What do you think this means?

For instance, you might have drawn a jigsaw puzzle scattered in disarray over a surface. You might have written words such as 'guilt', 'regret', 'disbelief', 'numb' and 'awed' on the actual jigsaw pieces. On the surface, around the jigsaw pieces, you might have written words like 'anger', 'hurt', 'powerless' and 'tortured'.
In this instance, the latter words formed part of the big picture and the former ones were part of the smaller picture. In her hurt, one client felt disbelief and in her powerlessness she felt guilt.

If you are artistically inclined, perhaps you might like to sculpt or make something that is symbolic of your grief. This idea of art symbolising grief is another way of picturalising your most intense innermost feelings.

It is one way of expressing your emotions. It is an alternative way, or a complementary one to speaking about your grief.

Do what feels right for you.

Tomas, a man in his 30s, who had lost his wife and children in a boating accident, was handy and before this tragedy had sculpted as a 'form of therapy' for himself. For many months after his loss, he was unable to do anything creative. He said he had felt 'immobilised'. However, one day he said he went out to the shops with the intention of getting 'something soft to mould'. He came back with play dough and spent a frenzied evening 'moulding it in the shape of my pain'.

Remember: There is no right way to express your grief feelings. As long as you can express them, that's the right way for you.

THE IMPORTANCE OF CLAIMING – OR RECLAIMING – YOUR GRIEF

It isn't until we can name – and thereby claim, or perhaps reclaim our grief that we can start to work on mending and healing our hearts. So think about how you can claim – or reclaim your grief.

Each loss is unique and each loss contains ties to past losses. Making the links between the past and the present – and doing your grief-work to resolve all your losses is the goal.

Ask yourself: what feelings and reactions do I have about my significant losses?

Talk about it out loud to someone supportive. Visualise yourself and your grief. Picturalise your grief – and draw it. Play with some clay. Do anything that helps you claim your feelings – and begin the grief-work process.

———————————

3

THE END
AND THE BEGINNING

'Grief is itself a med'cine.'

WILLIAM COWPER [1731-1800]

L ife is a continuous series of beginnings and endings that follow each other seamlessly, most of the time. The sun rises and sets. A school year begins and ends. Life is punctuated by starts and stops. The changes heralded by beginnings and endings may be almost imperceptible or they may be life-changing.

Many of these stops and starts are marked by celebration and formal tradition. New Year's Day, May Day, Thanksgiving mark the movement of one season to another. Religious holidays like Christmas, Hanukkah, Passover, Good Friday and Easter symbolise important beginnings and endings for spiritual and faith reasons.

Most of the beginnings and endings we experience in life happen seemingly naturally. We may be challenged and tested in our ability to adapt and grow as human beings. As we move from childhood to adolescence to adulthood and throughout our adult life, we change our values and beliefs, purpose and priorities. Much of this occurs imperceptibly. We leave behind our youthful exuberance and find wisdom as our hopes and dreams are tested by reality.

However, when these beginnings and endings are major ones, our sense of hope and promise in the change may turn to fear and trepidation. When we experience a major loss, we might see the spectre of the ending, but not the potential of a new beginning.

Yet, an ending heralds a beginning. And contained within an ending is a new beginning. We might resist this knowledge, but an ending provides us with an opportunity. From an ending can flow a beginning. An old proverb states, 'Every ending is hard'. The same might be said of every beginning.

In his book ***Living Your Dying***, Stanley Keleman says, *'Endings bring us face to face with the unknown. Endings force us to make new relationships, or at least offer the opportunity... Many people will say "that person is irreplaceable to me". The truth of the matter is that making an ending forces us to start being more self-reliant, or at least offers that opportunity.'*

At the intersection of an ending and a beginning lies the potential for an unchartered adventure. The promise of unknown hazards and unwelcome adventures might be scary. Yet it might also promise release from the pain. And a letting go which frees us to resume a new phase in our lives.

An ending and a beginning offer us the chance to re-evaluate our lives – and our destiny. No matter what the loss, the offer is there. However, before we can put some closure on the ending – in order to start our new beginning – we have to deal with our loss.

Loss is usually unexpected, unwanted and painful. Sometimes, denial is easier than doing the work of closure – and moving on to our new beginning.

But new beginnings cannot begin without closing the chapter on the ending. As Ross Goldstein, psychologist and author says,

> *'Saying good bye to an unrealistic image of yourself, to your dreams that haven't panned out, to career, to people – friends, spouses, parents – inherently carries pain. But you've got to say goodbye before you can say hello to whatever will be the next life structure that you're looking at.'*

Before you can begin again – you need to put closure on your grief – by doing your grief-work. However, for some people, denial gets in the way.

THE DENIAL OF GRIEF

Because loss means pain, we may try to avoid it – either consciously or unconsciously. We might try to protect ourselves from the ugly reality of our loss. Too often, people believe that, in order to disguise their pain, they need to hide their emotions – from even themselves.

Denying our feelings is something we might believe is the socially acceptable way to behave. After all, breaking down, or falling apart is too dangerous. Better to control your behaviour and have people believe you're coping. But at what cost? An appearance of strength can be just that – an appearance. The turmoil behind the façade might eventually create more problems in the future, than simple expression of the present pain.

What we need to recognise is that before any healing can occur, we need to allow ourselves to fall apart and experience our loss. It is only through experiencing our loss that we can accept it, face it and move back into life again. However, the pain that is an inherent part of loss is something we might want to avoid at all costs. We might even pretend to ourselves – and to others – that it doesn't exist. By protecting ourselves from the harsh, uncomfortable reality, often without being aware of what we're doing, we often can go to great lengths devising ways to deny our feelings.

Our denial might stem from our perceived need to 'stay together for others'. We believe we can't afford the luxury of 'falling apart' because other people would feel uncomfortable around us. We might fear that our distress and our tears will open old wounds for other people.

Related to this 'holding together for others' idea is that of 'the strength trap'. In an effort to appear strong some people might believe that giving in to falling apart will mean others pitying them – or judging them – for their weakness.

Denise, a 43-year-old woman, whose husband suddenly and unexpectedly left her for another woman spoke of her need to 'be strong'. She says,

'Life must go on. I get out – I mean what's the point of just sitting around the home and crying. I don't want to feel sorry for myself. Everyone tells me if I keep busy, I'll hurt less. So I'm getting my act together.'

Later on, Denise apologised for 'breaking down' in front of me. I had asked, 'Is it working?' She admitted that the need to be strong trapped her. She continues,

'No – It's not working. I feel like my whole life is one act. Michael leaving me just about devastated me. I feel sick a good deal of the time. Not physically sick but, unwell. I'm drinking too much. I know it, but it's the only way I can keep going. I feel like I'm in a trap. I'm torn between my grief and people practically insisting I 'get on with it.' My best friend is always saying, 'Life must go on.' I drink so I can cope.'

The strength trap was beginning to harm Denise. Fortunately, she came to realise it and decided to do something. She decided to stop buying into the message of 'life must go on' and mature people 'hold themselves together' and 'stay busy'. She knew the strength trap was hurting her. She decided she couldn't self-medicate with alcohol anyone. She decided to face her feelings. Denise resolved to begin the healing and mending process by facing her frightening feelings – and falling apart.

Submerging your grief in order to obey the messages of friends and society is harmful. Falling apart in the face of grief is not a weakness. Ultimately, it proves to be the strongest thing a grieving person can do.

Generally speaking, we live in a culture that warns us against 'wallowing in pity', or 'feeling sorry for ourselves'. Even expressions of loss and sorrow are put in negative terms:

falling apart	getting hysterical
breaking down	acting crazy
acting like a baby	losing your mind

It is easy to see how these negative expressions and messages can feed the grieving person's wish to avoid the pain. Such messages can lead to delayed grief. We all need to learn that sad behaviour is acceptable and will not necessarily result in disapproval from others.

Back in 1965, Geoffrey Gorer wrote, *'Mourning is treated as if it were a weakness, a self-indulgence, a reprehensible bad habit instead of a psychological necessity'*. It seems that very little has changed in the intervening years.

Catherine M. Sanders, PhD, writing from her extensive clinical and research experience in **Grief: The Mourning After**, gives the following account of one female respondent, a 55-year-old widow. As she struggled to get through the ritual at the graveside,

> *'I learned, as my mother before me, that you focus on something, and this is how you get through funerals. Like up to the cemetery, they had this artificial grass and I was really concentrating on the tricks the sun was playing on it. When the chaplain called me, he wanted to know if I had some personal things said and I said, "Oh, good Lord no". I said he had better keep it as impersonal as possible, otherwise we would need hip boots to get out of there... because his sister, I know, everybody would have started bawling. And so, he read the 23rd Psalm and something else, but it was very lovely.'*

So, because of the pain, grief is denied. The grieving person may feel embarrassed, even ashamed, if they show their feelings publicly. And it might make other people around them feel uncomfortable. Displaying emotions is out-of-control behaviour.

Catherine M. Sanders continues her analysis, based on the above quote and others from her Tampa study. She writes, *'The bereaved wish to maintain the appearance of strength during public rituals – perhaps because Americans place a high value on emotional control. Yet for some, this is impossible. They break down and, as a result, feel embarrassed, even shameful. The underlying message suggests that public displays of emotion are a breach of etiquette, even un-American... It is as though there is an unwritten dictum that states, "Thou shalt not grieve in public places".'*

The same dictum might be applied to grief generated by any other sort of loss. For instance, a male client once told me that the grief he suffered when his wife walked out on him – leaving him with their three children, was possibly greater than if she had died. He said, *'With death, it would be final. But not only was I shocked by what she'd done, I kept thinking,*

how am I going to live with the – I don't know how to express this – the guilt,
the shame, the anger, the rejection. And I just knew that most people would be
so uncomfortable saying anything to me – well, what could they say?
Sorry to hear your wife walked out on you? Sorry to hear she left you for
another man? I got some support because of the kids, but I didn't get much
emotional support myself. I was made to feel I should just get on with it.
That I wasn't to show how I really felt.'

GRIEVING TAKES ENORMOUS ENERGY

It is difficult to comprehend that a large part, if not every aspect of our life,
has changed profoundly. We need to realise that it takes enormous energy
to cope with our emotional suffering and the pain of acknowledging that
familiar patterns in life and connections with people have been irrevocably
altered. We may fear that we cannot salvage any parts of our old familiar life.
We feel anguish over the death of our hopes and dreams. Trying to heal
ourselves and getting on with our lives can be a battle.

Healing our wounded hearts is not something that can be left to chance.
Certainly time can help us, in offering us the time to heal ourselves. Time
alone, will not heal us. Mending and healing our hearts means facing
uncertainty and taking risks. In the face of the challenge of sorting out our
roles, expectations and motivations, we might feel discouraged. But, our loss
will forever remain if we don't muster the intention and will power in a
conscious decision to work towards getting better.

There is no doubt that grief is a difficult load to bear. Grief, however,
can be its own medicine as William Cowper suggests in the quote at
the beginning of this chapter. For while grief is an unhappy experience,
it can be constructive. In **Macbeth**, Shakespeare, through the characters of
Macbeth and the Doctor lets the reader know that grief is indeed 'its own
med'cine', if only Lady Macbeth will allow herself to succumb to it:

> Doctor: Not so sick, my lord,
>   As she is troubled with thick-coming fancies,
>   That keep her from rest,

Macbeth:	Cure her of that.
	Canst thou not minister to a mind diseas'd,
	Pluck from the memory a rooted sorrow,
	Raze out the written troubles of the brain,
	And with some sweet oblivious antidote
	Cleanse the stuff'd bosom of that perilous stuff
	Which weigh upon the heart?
Doctor:	Therein the patient
	Must minister to himself.

Macbeth, Act V, Scene iii

Grief helps us survive our loss. At the very best, it can be instructive. It can reward us with better self-understanding and a new perspective on life. In the long-term, grief can actually enhance our sense of self, because we know we have suffered, and we know we have survived.

For Cecily, a 14-year-old girl, unsure of herself, a little shy and going through the teenage girl's dilemma of 'Am I pretty enough?', "Am I slim enough?' and 'Am I popular enough?', her parents' separation and subsequent divorce produced a grief experience of profound proportions. When I saw Cecily, she had been living with her mother for eight months. She had minimal contact with her father. She was an only child, a child who had had a close relationship with her father. When her mother left her father, she went with her. Although Cecily had expressed a desire to live with her dad, his work situation, combined with her mother's determination to keep her former husband's influence to a minimum, ensured that Cecily stayed with her mother. As far as Cecily was concerned, she had lost her father. She says,

'I hardly get to see my dad. It's like he's died. But, it's really harder this way. Because if he'd really died, I guess I'd be able to let go. The way it is now, I feel like I should let go, but I know he's still around and I want to have him in my life, only I can't. Sometimes I get confused and mad about it.'

Cecily's comments tell us of the pain of separation and loss and highlight the idea of separations as being experienced like a 'little death'.

FACTORS WHICH HELP AND HINDER GRIEVING

Having the knowledge of what can help and hinder our grieving can assist us in our quest towards good grief.

Let's look at five features that can affect an individual's experience of grieving:

(a) personal life history
(b) personal family history
(c) gender
(d) age
(e) cultural beliefs

Because we are all unique, we have our own biographical history in our own family. How we have seen others around us deal with loss and change will affect, to some extent, our own coping strategies. We all grow up with role-models, yet we are also different individuals, so we might take on board an amalgam of the different coping styles we've observed in significant adults in our lives. In addition to this, societal attitudes to how girls and boys and women and men should behave in the face of loss and change will have an effect on how we believe we can express any distress we might feel. Tempering all this is the age at which we find ourselves dealing with the significant loss and change.

Generally speaking, younger individuals will have less experience of coping with adversity than older people. However, personality factors will also affect our responses. A shy and retiring younger person might have greater difficulty in expressing her pain than a similar age young woman who feels comfortable in ventilating her feelings and speaking openly about her grief. Cultural beliefs act as an overarching feature in how we deal with loss and change. If we live in a culture that values directness and openness and acknowledges the importance of ritual and putting closure on our grief experiences, we will be more encouraged to express and deal with our grief.

To highlight these factors, let's look at a case of grief as end and beginning. The following excerpt demonstrates all five factors: personal life history, family life history, gender, age and cultural beliefs.

The case to reflect upon is that of the author, Ruth Park. Her experience dates back to 1959. Since that time, there have been a number of changes in societal attitudes and growth in awareness of the importance of understanding grief issues. Nevertheless, it is a powerful case study.

The following excerpt comes from the autobiography of Ruth Park, whose husband, writer D'Arcy Niland, died suddenly of a heart condition. In this extract, Ruth Park recollects her experience.

'Sitting in a taxi, one freezing July day in 1959, I looked at my shoes and realised I had never seen them before. This seemed a mild curiosity and I stared at them for some time before I became aware that I did not know who I was, where I was going, whence I had come. So many years later I still quake when I remember the horror of that moment. It was a plain panic I suppose, my mind as disabled as my body. In such an experience, all the boundaries of one's little life are gone. One is standing on nothing in the middle of nothing.

I made up my mind that if I didn't recall my identity when the ferry reached Manly, I would ask where the police station was and find help. The decision calmed me; I sat quietly until the vessel began to lift on the swell crossing the Heads, and all in a moment, I knew who I was, I knew where I had been.

I was on my way home from hospital where I had left my husband in an intensive care ward. He had had a severe coronary occlusion and was in danger of another. By the time I reached home the phone might ring to tell me he was dead.

When my husband died I handled grief badly. People remarked on my calm or the capable manner in which I handled the innumerable complexities that follow a sudden death. I was unlikely to embarrass or distress them by weeping or throwing myself in front of a truck, and though their desire to console was genuine, they were secretly relieved.

'You've been wonderful,' they said.

To be wonderful is to handle grief badly. And so I nearly died. In a way I did die, as one might of shock after an amputation or a dreadful wound.

My own character and disposition made things worse for me, terribly worse. Reserve, independence and stoicism are not the qualities in grief. My sorrow when Merv my father died had taught me only one thing, that I could survive that sorrow. Not how to survive.

Our culture knows little about meeting grief head on. It has come to be our more most impregnable Tower of Babel, the very symbol of non-communication. We stand about it tears, wishing we could assuage the pain of persons dumbfounded by woe, but mostly we don't know what to say. Better to make no reference at all? Better, more tactful, to allow them to get over it in their own time?

It is all kindness, and no help. Thus entirely thrown upon oneself in a comfortless dark, one has the choice either of being wonderful or falling to pieces. And if you have children or others dependent on you, you cannot afford to fall to pieces. So mourning is not done, and the tears that run down inside turn to acid and that may corrode your soul for years.

You can't learn about bereavement, you can't teach anyone. It is like cold. You may inform a person who has never felt cold of every scientific fact – cause, consequence, attributes – but he will have no knowledge of cold until he experiences it.

So it is the fellow bereft who helps. Tears were beyond me, until an Italian shopkeeper, John Quatroville, who had suffered the loss of his baby daughter in a dreadful accident, took my hands and with speaking eyes gazed into my face. That was all. After that I was able to cry, but never where people could see me.

No one ever told me that the body grieves, slows down, its systems short circuit, that the immune system becomes so unstable you become a target for the so-called 'widows' syndrome'. The red vanished from my hair; in three weeks I was ash blonde. My teeth began rapidly to show small specks of decay. I expected any moment to hear two sharp snaps, as the arches of my feet gave way.'

Sydney Morning Herald: 30 October, 1993, 'Spectrum'

PROMPT FOR YOUR PEN

Exercise	Reflections on Ruth Park's experience

Reflect on Ruth Park's account. What does she tell you about her thoughts, feelings and behaviours? How does she account for what hindered her recovery? What does she say about what helped her? What hindered her?

Ruth Park's story tells us a number of important things about grief and its expression. First, we learn that grief is one of the most intense and powerful reactions we might ever experience in our lives. Of course, the intensity will depend on the circumstances. Ruth wrote about feeling shock, confusion that was so great it felt like madness and uncertainty regarding her identity and her purpose and location. She felt horror and panic and was immobilised by an inability to act. She felt lost and alone. Although she displayed an apparent calm, she also experienced an incapacity to show feelings and tears. Her grief manifested itself in a form of illness – her hair graying suddenly and evidence of tooth decay. Secondly, an individual's experience of grief will depend variously on factors associated with their particular life and the world in which they live. For instance, it could be said that what hindered Ruth's grief were her own personality and the lack of sensitivity and support from her friends. She says she was reserved and independent and therefore, unlikely to seek help easily. Her personal approach which was reserved, independent and 'brave' perhaps indicated that she had not learnt ways of coping well with grief. As she suggests, her grief in the past was of no help or instruction in the situation which faced her. Thirdly, a person's experience of grief will be affected by the prevailing societal views on the issue of death and dying. The response of those around Ruth was encouraging of denial and avoidance rather than the expression of painful feelings. Nevertheless, her recovery was helped by someone who had himself experienced grief and offered her recognition and support to express herself.

Since 1959, there have been advances in awareness regarding to need to experience grief. Nevertheless, some people might continue to experience the denial of grief in those around them, for as Ruth Park suggests, expressing grief openly can make some people around the grieving person very uncomfortable.

UNDERSTANDING GOOD GRIEF

Good grief involves a grieving process that helps to separate us from the past. Whether this separation is from a significant person in our lives, a relinquishing of a life which is no longer possible or adjustment to a new set of expectations or a different body image, the grieving process moves us onward and forward.

Good grief work involves the relinquishment of past connections and steps toward a new reality. Adapting J. William Worden's tasks of grieving to cover all types of losses, there are four tasks to be undertaken.

First, there is accepting the reality of the loss.

Secondly, there is the experiencing of the pain of grief.

Thirdly, there is the adjustment to the new reality in which the loss leaves a gap.

Fourthly, there is the withdrawal of emotional energy from the lost relationship, person, or part of yourself, and a reinvestment in the new reality.

Good grief means completing all four tasks.

However, good grief also means being aware that every individual has an unique timetable. We cannot compare ourselves to others. We cannot and should not attempt either to hurry the process along or to delay it. The prolonged use of sedatives can add to the risk of prolonging or blocking the good grief work that needs to be done.

Good grief is really 'normal' grief. Yet, few grieving people would call their response to the losses and changes they are experiencing 'normal'.

How can we tell the good from the bad when it comes to grief? As we have seen, good grief means experiencing pain and discomfort, even torment. By avoiding this pain, a person will not be able to move forward and recover.

Good grief brings with it the potential for recovery, growth and change and the opportunity to heal the emotional pain and move forward with life. All this is necessary if a grieving person is to adjust and build a new reality.

Bad grief, on the other hand, is the sort that is inadequate or incomplete. This sort of grief does not provide the opportunity to mature and change. It holds the person in emotional bondage. By being permanently shackled to old, unresolved issues, a person will be held in perpetual slavery – until they realise the benefits of going through the pain of good grief.

The 'unfinished business' of grief that is not done – which is not carried to completion is well exemplified in the story of Queen Victoria who grieved for her husband, Prince Albert as long as she lived. She was said to have ordered his clothes to be laid out each day, water set out for his shaving and everything was kept as he had left it. In Eugene Field's poem, **Little Boy Blue**, we read that the toys are kept forever, awaiting the little boy who has died.

In such instances, there is no acceptance by the people concerned that they must let go and recover from their grief. These people are said to be 'fixated' and they cannot move ahead with resolving their grief until they accept the reality and move beyond the attachment they felt – the emotional investment they had in the person now gone. They must learn to reinvest in a new reality.

Good grief recognises the end and the beginning. Good grief puts closure on the loss we have experienced and it opens us into a new phase of our lives.

With good grief, or 'normal' grief, the pain, distress, longing and emptiness decreases. The person eventually recovers and picks up the pieces of their life and forms new relationships. For some people, the experience of grief is very confronting, and many people report that their life has been enhanced by the experience. They say that they have been forced to reflect upon and consider the deeper meanings of life and surprisingly, at times, they discover unknown inner strengths and external supports that they believe will help them face future obstacles.

It is a truism that everyone will be changed in some way by a grief experience. Some people will be so overwhelmed by the experience that they deny aspects of it to themselves and they remain fixed in a state of grief. This was the case in the earlier example of Queen Victoria. This sort of grief may be called 'unresolved', 'obstructed', 'blocked', 'abnormal', 'pathological', 'complicated', 'chronic', or in keeping with the good grief terminology, might be called 'bad' grief.

Good grief is not indicated by signs and reactions different from bad grief. As indicated earlier, people experiencing good grief, talk about a greatly varied range of intense reactions, many of which feel very 'abnormal' or 'bad' to them. Feelings such as intense sadness, restlessness, confusion, preoccupation, sense of presence and searching behaviour are all experienced as deeply disturbing.

What differentiates good grief from bad grief is the persistence of the signs and reactions and the extent to which the grieving person can resume a meaningful and satisfying life.

It is the ability to adjust, change and recover over a period of time that makes grief good.

The following table shows differences between good and bad grief.

Normal or 'Good Grief' and Unresolved or 'Bad Grief'

Normal or good grief	Unresolved or bad grief
denial	endless denial
bodily distress	constant bodily distress
anger	enduring anger
idealisation*	unceasing idealisation
guilt	continued guilt
hostility	extended hostility
panic	persistent panic

Adapted from McKissock, 1983

* Idealisation here means an unrealistically positive view, where a person is not able to bring himself or herself to talk about any faults in the deceased.

71

Understanding the difference between normal and unresolved grief responses helps us determine how we might deal with our own experiences – and how we might help others cope better.

Some theorists have developed a stage model of grief. Elizabeth Kubler-Ross developed a five-stage model which she applied to the stages of dying. Others have adapted this model to working with grieving people.

1. **Denial** – which is really a resistance or avoidance. It is a way of protecting ourselves from something that is too frightening and painful. Most people eventually let the truth in, but in their own time and at their own pace. People move from a position of 'I don't believe this is happening' to 'I know this is happening, but I can't believe it'.

2. **Anger** – as a person accepts the reality of the situation, they are likely to feel angry. They feel angry and frustrated and irritated by the unfairness of life.

3. **Bargaining** – this manifests itself as an attempt to gain time and to delay the inevitable. Sometimes there is a bit of acceptance at this stage, but there is still an attempt to postpone or avoid matters.

4. **Depression** – a sad hopelessness sets in after the first emotional storms have passed. A person may feel apathetic and lethargic and may withdraw. This is a normal reaction, and is part of the movement of the person towards acceptance.

5. **Acceptance** – is the coming to terms with the loss and learning to live with it. This stage is often characterised by an absence of the powerful emotions that precede it. This acceptance is not meant to be a resignation, but a true, wholehearted acceptance.

There are some drawbacks to the idea of stages. It should be recognised that people do not necessarily experience the stages in this particular order. For instance, anger and sadness and depression may occur at any time. They may be felt more or less intensely, depending on the nature of the loss and the personality of the grieving individual. Some people may miss a stage.

Other people may pass through one or all of these stages faster than others or they may experience all of the stages, fluctuating from anger to denial to bargaining and around again. Others still may become 'stuck' at a particular stage, sometimes for years, for instance, they may be depressed for years.

These stages, while useful to understand, cannot be interpreted as rigid and immutable. As C. S. Lewis suggested, grief is a process that has its own timetable.

You might like to test your understanding of some of these stages. Look at the following exercise and answer the questions at the end.

Exercise   Janis Ian song: 'Jesse Come Home'

The following lyrics are taken from Janis Ian's **Stars** album. The music is evocative and the lyrics tell us a lot about the writer – and singer's – feelings.

Jesse come home, there's a hole in the bed
where we slept
now it's growing cold.
Jesse your face in the place where we lay
Try the hearth all apart it hangs on my heart
And I'm leaving the light on the stairs
No I'm not scared I'll wait for you

Hey Jesse it's lonely come home
Jesse the stairs and the halls they are calling you stay
And I remember too
All the pictures are shaded and fading in gray
And I still set a place at the table at noon
And I'm leaving a light on the stairs
No I'm not scared I'll wait for you
I'll wait for you
Hey Jesse it's lonely come home

Jesse the spread on the bed it's like when you left
I kept it for you
All the blues and the greens have been recently cleaned
And are seemingly new
Hey Jesse me and you will swallow the light on the stairs
I'll fix up my hair we'll sleep unaware
Hey Jesse it's lonely come home.

PROMPT FOR YOUR PEN

Exercise	Reflections on the song and songwriter's emotional state

What are the songwriter's thoughts and feelings?
Reflect on the songwriter's experience of grief in terms of the five stage model of grief.

Janis Ian's lyrics tell us of her intense longing and yearning for the lost partner. She sings of her sadness, emptiness and loneliness and her preoccupation with being reunited. She is yearning for peace in 'sleep unaware'. There are aspects of denial, in the reluctance to accept the loss as real: 'Jesse your face in the place where we lay'. There is no acceptance yet of the finality of the loss. Ideas of reunion have not been put aside, because she is still setting, 'a place at the table at noon', 'leaving a light on the stairs' and keeping the place as the lost partner would have liked.

It is important to remember that acceptance of loss does not necessarily have to be complete for people to make an adjustment to a new reality. For instance, in the song **Jesse Come Home**, the lyrics might be expressing how the writer and singer feels only some of the time. The yearning and sadness seem to indicate an earlier stage of grief, however, it depends on how the writer is able to function generally in her life and the extent to which the feelings expressed in the song affect her life. Do they dominate her life? Are they present only sometimes? At night? On week-ends? Does she accept the reality of the loss? Can she adjust to a new reality?

TOWARDS NEW MODELS OF GRIEF

More recently, theorists have put forward new models of grief, which are not as seemingly fixed as the stage models. These newer models examine two different ways of viewing grief, which are not necessarily opposed.

Two such models explore:

(a) phases of grief
(b) tasks of grieving

Model: Phases of grief

The phases model, developed by Margaret Miles, suggests that there are three phases. This model can be depicted as follows:

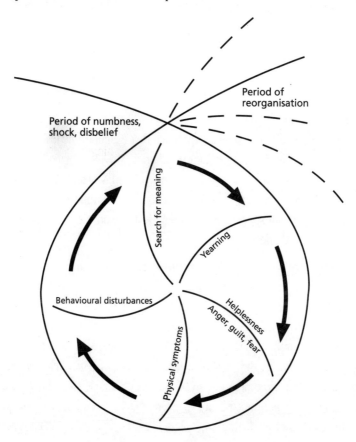

First, there is a phase in which there is a person experiences a period of numbness, shock and denial. In the second phase, a person may experience a period of intense sadness, however, there can be great variations and changes in this time – there is no progression through a set series of stages – and feelings. Rather, a person may go back and forth in their feelings and may have several seemingly contradictory feelings occurring simultaneously. For example, a person may feel emptiness, fear and anger at the same time. Such mixed feelings can be experienced as coming in waves. When these waves of mixed feelings drop in intensity and there is a longer interval between the waves, people might feel they are on the road to recovery. The third phase is a period of recovery and reorganisation. There is no one exit point. Some people may benefit from their experience and emerge from their grief with new insights, an improved level of functioning and gains in emotional growth. They have experienced good grief. Others may not emerge so soundly and may not feel they have acquired adequate coping skills. These people might be vulnerable to losses in the future.

Model: Tasks of grieving

Another model of grief offers an approach that examines the tasks a grieving person undertakes to achieve their good grief.

The following model is based on the work of J. William Worden. While it might appear to be the case that this model presupposes that a person performs tasks in a specific order, in reality, a person can be working on all four tasks at the one time.

The first task: is the acceptance of the loss. This is the first – and a big task. Very often, we can understand that there has been a loss, we have an intellectual realisation of the loss, however, it is difficult to fully accept the loss on an emotional level. It is this deeper, emotional level that contains the recognition that the loss is irrevocable. At the beginning of the first task, there may be a denial of the loss. The grieving person may refer to their lost partner, relationship or loss of part of self, yet be unable to acknowledge the loss. This denial is protective, it is a strong defence against the unknown.

In good grief-work, the two phases of the first task: intellectual and emotional acceptance may coincide or they may follow each other. In grief work that has complications, people may come to a halt in both the first and the second phase of the first task.

The second task: working through the emotions of grief. Working through the emotions of grief is painful. It means not avoiding or denying the intense pain of grief. Working through the pain means staying with the strength of feeling associated with sadness, yearning, anger, fear and guilt. The idea of society's 'rules' constraining the grieved person applies here. There are expectations regarding how people are allowed to express their feelings and for how long. However, it is wise to remember the old adage: 'if you want to heal, first you must feel'. Working through emotions means staying with the feelings and acknowledging them so that eventually they begin to lessen in intensity.

The third task: acquiring new skills. Following the first two tasks of grief-work – accepting that loss is final and dealing with the feelings that arise from this acceptance – is acquiring new skills in coping with your new life. This involves both contacts with other people and accomplishing practical tasks. Your beliefs and values about the world are challenged and your task is to adjust to your new context. Some people report that they have lost direction in their lives. The good grief-work involved in undertaking the third task means finding the motivation to adjust to the changes and becoming self-confident enough to test out new, and sometimes forgotten old, skills.

Moving successfully through this third task can result in personal growth. By knowing you can meet new challenges and cope with changes, you may gain in self-confidence and a sense of self-fulfillment. By not rising to the challenges, a person withdraws and might well feel more anxious and less confident about their sense of place in the world.

The fourth task: reinvesting emotional energy. This final task entails understanding that good grief means reinvesting your emotional energy in new relationships, new ways of being. In a sense, you have to be able to say good-bye to a loved one, a cherished role, an unfulfilled dream or a lost part of yourself, before you can say hello to other people and other ways of living your life. Your aim is to say farewell to the past and to discover and explore new experiences or old experiences that bring you a sense of joy and satisfaction.

GRIEF IS WORK

Whether you are drawn to a stages approach or a phases and tasks approach to grief work, what you will have discovered is that grief involves work. It means actively working through pain and loss. This idea of grief as work might help you understand that although you feel helpless and powerless, you do have some control over how you choose to deal with your grief. You will know that grief is not something that just eases with the passage of time but rather a process which needs to be actively entered into – giving yourself over to getting in touch with your coping skills and adjusting to changes.

Another advantage of grief-work is that actively grieving may provide an opportunity or challenge for you to gain insight and understand yourself better. You might be surprised at what you have gained in the process – wisdom, self-knowledge and understanding of your place in the world. Of course, when you are still grieving, it might be hard to see any advantages or potential gains. You might have that revelation later – often much later.

Grieving is work and through grief-work we can find resolution. Gwendolyn Brooks summed this up in the lines:

Beware the easy griefs
that fool and fuel nothing.

['Boys, Black' Beckonings, 1975]

PROMPT FOR YOUR PEN

Exercise **In retrospect**

There are many influences in all our lives that can affect how we behave and respond in any given situation. Spend some time reflecting on your past.

• What influences can you remember from your formative years that might prevent you from expressing your sadness, your grief?

• Do you still think and behave in any ways that no longer serve you in your efforts to get in touch with your sadness and your grief?

What would you need to do to move forward?

———————————

PART II

THE MANY
FACES OF GRIEF

'There are many griefs so loud
They could bring down the sky,
And there are griefs so still
None knows how deep they lie.

MAY SARTON [Of Grief]

4

INCIDENTAL AND INEVITABLE LOSSES, AND LIFE'S LET-DOWNS

For the first time, I was pierced by the little panic
and tristesse occasioned by small things passing
irrevocably from view.

FAITH SULLIVAN [The Cape Ann, 1988]

Whenever we must bid farewell to one kind of life and greet the arrival of another – there is the potential for change, growth – and loss. Puberty, the menopause, ageing are examples of three phases that contain the elements of physical and emotional challenges. They are markers of change in our lives. Most people move through this process of being challenged by a new period of life – a developmental phase – quietly and successfully. Perhaps those people who do not fare so well do not realise that some grief-work is required. Adjustments are called for by the changes that visit us in these developmental phases. The young person must give up their childhood identity, their sense of security in being a child without the responsibilities and demands that adolescence inevitably brings. With adolescence comes more responsibility, more pressures and stresses – and a new identity crisis to be worked through. The safe child must undergo metamorphosis to become the emerging adolescent, with a new set of expectations and sense of self in the world. The adolescent may feel the losses acutely. Perhaps the changes they are moving through represent the loss of innocence and a relatively carefree existence. Whatever the perceived losses for the individual teenager, the transition from child to teenager is symbolic of losses – and gains.

DEVELOPMENTAL PHASES AND GRIEF-WORK

At critical phases in life, we often are puzzled by feeling confused and contrary to how we believe we should feel. Growing up, getting married, having children, going through the menopause, retirement and ageing often entail inevitable losses: the loss of freedom, the farewell to old roles, dreams, involvement and excitement – and new challenges and choices that we may not wish to face. We often feel 'let-down'. Sometimes we resist that change and resent the loss.

THE DILEMMA OF GROWING UP

For most young girls and boys 'growing up' can provide new challenges and exciting possibilities. Some pre-teens can't wait to grow up and earn more independence and freedom. For them the losses are outweighed by the exciting gains of being a teenager. Of course, they all face the identity redefinitions – and sometimes, the crisis of answering the important questions: 'Who am I?' and 'What's it all about?' However, for some young people, growing up can be a painful reminder of losses – and as yet, untested potential gains. Sherry, a 14-year-old girl was not moving into her new identity with ease. In her case it was a downright struggle. She resented what she called 'growing up pressures' and was very direct about her intentions. She wanted to remain a child for as long as possible. Sherry was unable to accept the need to change. She did not accept the reality of the loss of childhood – and she got stuck in her grief-work. Sherry was referred for depression and an eating disorder. An intelligent girl, she was honest about her dilemma – and she had great insight into her attitude and behaviour. She simply refused to grow up. Growing up for Sherry represented untold dangers and a life she could not see herself living. She was adamant she did not want a relationship and the thought of settling down and having children was anathema to her. Hers was a conservative family background and she had heard messages relating to how her life should turn out 'since I was a little girl'. She rejected these messages – and expectations. In her desperation to not confront the beginnings of a life course she dreaded, she became withdrawn, depressed and her eating disorder meant she was keeping herself 'small and slim'. She wanted to cling to a more vulnerable identity that she saw adolescence would strip from her. She says,

'I don't want to go there. It's too scary. I can see what happens to people when they grow up. They change. I don't want to do that. Everyone keeps saying I'll get over it – but to me – it feels like I want to stay here. I feel safe. I can't cope with the idea of too much pressure.'

Sherry is implying that the price of growing up is too high. It brings with it too many dangers and pitfalls. Sherry needs to grieve what she is leaving behind and accept the reality of change. Her parents confirmed that Sherry was sensitive to changes and pressures, and that her asthma would flare if she felt 'stressed'. They had become despairing, because they claimed that no amount of 'good sense' and talking by them had helped shift Sherry in her point of view. How does a girl like Sherry get 'unstuck'? Not easily, in her case. It was only after one hospitalisation for her eating disorder and another for an attempted suicide that Sherry came to realise moving through a critical phase of life – a developmental phase must be completed satisfactorily if life is to proceed.

Of course, most children successfully negotiate their adolescence. However, adolescence is a time of great changes and emotional turmoil. Sherry is right in her assumption that 'growing up' can be fraught with unknown hazards. Growing up means leaving behind our childhood image of ourselves and finding a new identity. In his classic book,

Childhood and Society, the famous psychoanalyst, Erik Erikson, described the core task of adolescence as that of establishing a sense of identity. It is in the adolescent years that we become aware of having a separate and unique existence yet a sense of belonging to and identifying with a family, peer groups and society.

Dylan Thomas in his poem, **Fern Hill**, captures the happiness and laughter of childhood:

> *And as I was green and carefree, famous among the barns*
> *About the happy yard and singing as the farm was home,*
> *In the sun that is young once only,*
> *Time let me play and be*
> *Golden in the mercy of his means,*
> *And green and golden I was huntsman and herdsman, the calves*
> *Sang to my horn, the foxes on the hills barked clear and cold,*
> *And the sabbath rang slowly*
> *In the pebbles of the holy streams.*
>
> *And honored among foxes and pheasants by the gay house*
> *Under the new made clouds and happy as the heart was long,*
> *In the sun born over and over,*
> *I ran my heedless ways,*
> *My wishes raced through the house high hay*
> *And nothing I cared, at my sky blue trades, that time allows*
> *In all his tuneful turning so few and such morning songs*
> *Before the children green and golden*
> *Follow him out of grace.*

Judith Viorst in **Necessary Losses** describes how some children are not ready to 'grow up'. For the fictional Peter Pan, refusing to grow up, this ploy may work. But for the 11-year-old girl who tells her mother, *'I'll never want to go out with a boy. Don't ever think I'll want to wear lipstick and make-up or anything either!'* the writing is on the wall.

All children must be led out of grace and into adolescence.

FACING 'THE CHANGE'

In ancient times, when women of the tribe reached menopause, it was a sign of honour, respect and wisdom. Generally speaking, in our youth-dominated society, this is not the case today. However, with more and more Baby Boomers reaching their midlife years, the taboos around talking about menopause have been lifted. In fact, there is a deluge of information available in books, magazines and videos about 'managing your menopause'.

The menopause, or what is often colloquially called 'the change' is Nature's fact of life. All women must pass through it, sooner or later.

Around the menopause, some women develop a state resembling chronic grief, because there are reminders seemingly all around them of their losses. Contextually, the midlife woman must contend with many changes, challenges and losses. Some women can articulate the losses they are facing and be confident that there will be gains as she enters a new cycle of life. For others, the losses loom large and the gains are not substantial enough to offer compensation. In fact, for these women, the very need to accept changes and the reality of making adjustments is impossible. So, these women often deny the reality and continue behaving as if they are untouched by change and loss.

An adaptive attitude was expressed by Thelma, 50, who clearly had done her grief-work around 'the change'. Her sense of humour comes through when she says,

> *'I'm pretty happy with myself now. I'm not the girl I used to be, but I'm a very confident woman. I've grown up. I don't believe in fairy tales anymore. There are no more frogs and no more princes for me.'*

MEN AND THE 'MALE MENOPAUSE'

Women often joke about their men 'going through the male menopause' when they find him speaking or behaving in distinctly uncharacteristic ways. The man who has never more than looked at other women might begin making suggestive comments – or acting on fantasies hitherto forbidden by his own code of honour. Similarly, men who have never been particularly vain might begin to obsess about their hairline or sexual staying power and prowess.

I've known women who rationalise such behaviour and even go along with new ideas and schemes that would have horrified them only weeks earlier. They are forgiving – and even find their men's new ways fetching. One woman commented half-jokingly, half-seriously: *'He's such a devil. He told me that he'd reached that time of life when it was either a new woman – or a new car. I guess you'll have to have the new car I said.'* The new car to which this woman was agreeing, was not your average new car – but an imported, sleek sports-car worth a lot of money.

Ross Goldstein in **Fortysomething** reminds us why such thinking and behaviour might be common in the midlife years:

'The three big wake-up calls of midlife are disconcerting. They include the realizations that, one, you're not going to become president of the company (or, if you are president, it's not as much fun as you thought it would be); two, your family is never going to look like Ozzie and Harriet's; and three, you're not going to live forever.'

Essentially, what the midlife male might be responding to by behaving uncharacteristically – are losses – and perceived losses. Changes and shifts need to be made – and sometimes, the man's ego is not ready to accept the soul-crafting necessary at midlife. He doesn't want to reorganise priorities – he might just want to hang on to the memory of youth with all its trappings of a fun and carefree existence. What better way of doing this but in the stereotypical – and cliched manner – to find a youthful woman and/or a car to remind him of his youth.

Many years ago, when I was less familiar with these dynamics, I was surprised by the number of women who encouraged their partner's new quirks – either directly or indirectly. One female client confessed that she felt compelled to accept her husband's behaviour because her own sense of security in the relationship was more important to her than her sense of pride. She didn't want to lose her husband – or the security he afforded her. She said,

'Since I've been married, I've led a comfortable life. I know he's seeing someone else – I'd have to be deaf, dumb and blind not to know. But I choose to not know. At least as far as any scene with him is concerned. You see, I'm frightened of losing him – it gets me down – hell, that's why I'm here now with you – but I have to accept that he is a free agent. At least I have to accept it if I want the security I get from being married to him.'

The security this woman referred to was not insignificant. A lovely house, an account to shop to her heart's content, her own car and late adolescent children still living at home – were all too much to lose. Although her situation 'got her down' and she experienced bouts of depression, her fear of loss outweighed her sense of dissatisfaction. At least at that point in time.

A situation where a couple experience in tandem 'menopause' was evidenced by Robert and Tracey, who came to counselling for their increasingly unhappy relationship. Both in their late forties, they believed their relationship was all but over and according to Robert, Tracey had started to 'nag' him and he was fed up. Tracey, on the other hand, thought the blame lay with Robert who had always been kind and attentive, until recently. Their relationship had deteriorated to the point where they had few kind words to say to each other and had stopped having sex. Robert blamed Tracey and her 'menopause' which he claimed made her moody and irritable. Tracey blamed Robert's 'male menopause' which she saw manifesting itself in his more than usual amount of looking at other women and a new tendency to dress 'young'. In fact, Tracey admitted in their counselling that she believed Robert was having an affair. He denied this allegation hotly, adding, *'But who could blame me? You're making life very difficult for us both.'*

It took three counselling sessions to reveal that their combined 'menopause' symbolised a number of losses. Their difficulty in facing these and adjusting to the necessary changes, made them vulnerable to strains and tensions in their relationship. It transpired that Tracey had suffered three miscarriages in their seventeen year marriage and after the last one had been told that she could not have children. This loss had not been worked through and remained unresolved. Their plans to adopt had not been successful, and even overseas adoption had been ruled out on the basis of age. Tracey and Robert had not faced or grieved these losses in any meaningful way. Tracey said, *'It seemed too hard to face up to each blow...it was easier to just keep going and not look back'*. This tendency to 'not look back' had led them to a point where pent-up emotions and unresolved feelings were trickling out in the form of irritability, resentment, regret, guilt and depression. Their individual and joint unconscious decisions to 'not look back' was having a profoundly negative effect on their relationship. It was not until they had decided it was imperative to 'look back' that we could move forward in counselling and healing the wounds of past losses.

LOSS AND GRIEF IN AGE

The proportion of those over 65 in the population, is increasing steadily. Medical advances and sound public health policy have played a large part in helping us live longer. Despite such advances and improved living conditions, the biological process of ageing still continues and with it, the often uncomfortable feeling the older person has when he or she looks in the mirror every morning.

Ageing is, in itself, deeply disturbing to some people. It is a state generally undervalued in the world, with some exceptions in cultures where respect is paid to those who have accrued wisdom through a long life. But, for many in the Western world, old age is dreaded and for some certainly delayed as long as possible.

With age, the multiplicity of losses include physical, psychological, social and cultural ones. Some of these are connected. For instance, a loss of health may cause loss of strength, loss of mobility and loss of independence. In its most extreme form, a loss of memory leads inevitably to a loss of almost everything else.

Elderly people, sometimes are fearful of expressing their feelings of loss and grief. Often they do so by way of a 'joke'. However, we all know that humour masks our fears and is often more telling than a direct remark. Older people will sometimes say things like, 'Well, at my age...' or 'I guess that sort

of thing happens with age', or 'It's my age, you know', by way of explanation
– or excuse for something they feel they've 'done wrong' or feel 'blamed for'.
Along with the obvious feelings and fears are the hidden fears of ageing.
These are related to loss of freedom and independence and the regression
to a child-like state that are the consequences of some physical and mental
conditions.

PROMPT FOR YOUR PEN

Exercise	Hierarchy of need and corresponding losses

If you were asked to construct a hierarchy of needs and corresponding losses,
where would aged people assign the various capabilities and the losses of these:

• loss of independence
• loss of self-esteem
• loss of mobility
• loss of speech
• loss of memory
• loss of significant people through moving away or death
• loss of hearing
• loss of sight
• loss of strength
• loss of general health

Reflect on your hierarchy.
Why have you constructed your hierarchy as you have?
What does it say about your perception of needs and losses?

GRIEVING FOR OURSELVES IN AGE

Age realistically is a time of loss and separation – from our younger and
midlife selves. The experience of loss of energy levels, loss of sexual
prowess, loss of physical strength and actual muscle mass, changes in skin
texture, both quantitative and qualitative hair loss – can't be denied. At the
same time, our society's emphasis on youth and beauty makes the reality

of ageing even more difficult to accept. There are no culturally accepted and recognised methods of grieving the real loss of youth and all it means and provides.

That's why it's important to look out for yourself – and after yourself, by understanding that ageing inherently involves your doing your grief-work.

Not everyone has the same difficulty in accepting the markers of age. We have all met eighty-year olds who can realistically talk of what they've lost, perhaps with a touch of nostalgia, and about their limited life ahead – and yet be happy. These are the people who have done their grief-work. These are not the people who have tried to deny their losses, continued to 'act young' and wanted to fool everyone – unsuccessfully.

Only when we accept the reality of loss can we build a satisfactory life. In a sense, our ability to grow and change, to remain flexible in our outlook is 'youthful'. By adopting such an outlook, we can look forward to the promise of new satisfactions and new interests as long as we live.

LOSING OUR MATERIAL POSSESSIONS

If it is true that mere 'things', items and possessions mean nothing, then why do many people feel so much grief when a new car is wrecked or their house is burgled and jewellery they have inherited goes missing? Why do these things matter so in our lives?

Of course, our common sense tells us that mere 'things' – material possessions can be replaced. We have insurance to enable us to replace valuables lost or destroyed.

Yet, we all know that the things we value most can't be replaced, and even if they can, the symbolic value of the originals to us, cannot be replaced. The following possessions generally are considered to be of value:

- family photographs
- jewellery from previous generations
- presents from significant people – family and friends (often these can be trivial objects in themselves, but they are precious to us because they represent affection)

- our house which has so many memories of shared laughter and shared anxiety
- books which may by replaceable, but even if they are, the original copies carried special memories
- car, which is one of the most easily replaceable objects, may carry with it memories of occasions and experiences, otherwise why do so many people feel a sense of loss when they voluntarily trade in an old car for a new model?

PROMPT FOR YOUR PEN

Exercise	Objects of value to you

Think of 3 objects that might appear to an outsider to have no value, but which carry enormous symbolic value for you.
What is the symbolism of personal possessions?

Why should they matter so? Dr Beverley Raphael, psychiatrist and researcher, in her work on loss and grief discusses the relationship of possessions to losses sustained in Australian bush fires. She points out that even trivial objects can have profound emotional significance. For instance, to a family whose house was totally destroyed, even small fragments of roof-tile was observed to bring a sense of comfort.

Security may be represented in a variety of objects, the security blanket for the child, the house or bank account to an older person. Some people have kept every bank statement of the early years of their marriage as a reminder of the progress of the relationship, from past financial precariousness to present comfort or even prosperity. One wealthy older woman told me she still wears her simple diamond engagement ring because 'it reminds me of how poor and happy we were.' Her husband has offered to replace the simple ring with a more expensive version, but this woman won't agree to such a loss of their past.

> **PROMPT FOR YOUR PEN**

Exercise   What would you rescue?

Imagine your home was threatened by fire.
You know everyone is safe and out of the house.
You have one minute to leave the house.
What objects would you choose to carry from the fire?

Questions for reflection:
• What is the symbolism of your choice?
• What does it tell you about your priorities in life?

SYMBOLISM AND SECURITY

Many people probably would nominate photographs as their choice of object to rescue. Photographs have symbolic importance in security and relationships.

It is interesting to note that following a disastrous bush fire in South Australia in 1983, in which historical homesteads and properties were destroyed, families rallied together to share their remaining photographs. One family who had lost everything was given copies of photographs from another family's collection, showing the house and grounds as they used to be. It was a beginning in helping the devastated family to re-build their personal and family archives.

Our sense of security also is affected by illness and disability. In one sense, the walking frame for the stroke patient may seem to be symbolic of security, it may, in another sense, represent loss and act as a reminder of the changes in their life brought on by disability. When a therapist prescribes a prosthesis or aid to daily living, it is done with positive intentions, to assist the patient. However, the emotional impact of this is important to acknowledge. The patient may be ambivalent about the aid, which symbolises a loss.

For some people, status is an important aspect of their personal or family life. For others, it seems completely unimportant, of minor significance, or too trivial to be taken seriously. Many objects can be symbolic of status. The car you own and drive, the type of house in which you live, the clothes you wear, the title by which you are called and your general style of living have symbolic value in proclaiming yourself to the world and claiming your status in the hierarchy of society.

It is because of this strong symbolism that the loss of linked objects may cause a grief, which is, to the observer, totally disproportionate to the actual value of the objects lost.

The symbolism of the title by which one is called can be very important for some people. For a revered academic to be given the title 'Emeritus Professor' is an indication that the title, 'Professor' is, of itself, important. The person so bestowed can retain into retirement a sign to society of their importance and status.

Material objects are important to us all to some degree. However, to dispossessed people, the symbolism of material objects can far outweigh the value of the objects themselves. Australian Aboriginals concerned by the loss of their traditional sacred sites, are usually not thinking of the actual land value, but of what these areas represent in the Dreamtime. Cultural heritage is closely linked to the land and the very landscape of that land.

In every country where cultural imperialism has acted to devalue an age-old culture, there needs to be renewed recognition of the sense of loss and encouragement by society to revalue that grief and to make amends.

This sense of community loss and grief is often seen after natural disaster and war. There will be individual, family and whole community responses to the loss of material possessions. These material possessions will range from all important photographs to valuable historical buildings. The grief of the people of England, and particularly Coventry, was enormous when they lost their great Cathedral as a result of air raid destruction.

We should stop and reflect before we deride the loss of mere 'things'. Things can symbolise our personal relationships, our family connections, our past as well as our future in the community of our society.

Ellen Glasgow, in her 1902 work, **The Battle-Ground**, summed up material losses beautifully in the lines: *'She must face her grief where the struggle is always the hardest – in the place where each trivial object is attended by pleasant memories.'*

5

LOSING A PART
OF OURSELVES

O! Call back yesterday, bid time return.
WILLIAM SHAKESPEARE [Richard II]

I*t was the 29th of November. I'll never forget the date'.* These were
the first words spoken by Maria McCarthy at a forum entitled:
'Accidentally learning more about life'. Maria McCarthy was a
healthy and energetic woman of 41, a woman who had a good job,
a relationship – and a passion for jogging. She led what she called a 'pacy'
life and as she told the forum of grief counsellors, *'Ironically, it was weeks
before the accident that I started questioning life – is this how I want to live
my life?'* When, on the 29 November, she was hit by a car while jogging,
her life came to a grinding halt and over the next three years, her task
was *'rebuilding my world'.* Her injuries were severe – her bones were
broken in 20 places and she suffered extensive bruising and tissue damage.
Maria had double vision for over sixteen months, making her feel, *'As if
I wasn't on Planet Earth',* and her intensive rebuilding of her body and soul
was a three year journey…and is still continuing. Maria says,

> *'It sounds bizarre but I wouldn't change what's happened for all the tea in
> China. It was horrific, disgraceful, a nightmare. It's been imperative to admit
> how shocking it's been. But the accident has been great for me too.'*

In her powerful presentation, Maria spoke about the meaning of loss for her and the importance of grief. Maria's losses were related to loss of herself at every level: physical, psychological and social. With these multiple losses came loss of expectation, loss of role, loss of independence, loss of self-esteem, loss of mobility, loss of strength and loss of general health. In Maria's case, these losses were temporary, albeit lasting some years, however, in other people's cases, such losses following injury, may last a life-time.

Almost three years on, Maria says she's still 'not over it yet', but she is an enthusiastic, healthy woman committed to telling her story and helping other people understand the importance of grieving and its central place in the journey of self-discovery.

We tend to take our health and vitality for granted. It usually isn't until we lose our health, or witness someone else lose theirs, that we begin to realise the enormity of the loss.

WHEN OUR LOSSES CHALLENGE OUR RELATIONSHIP WITH OURSELVES

Our physicality is part of our human heritage. We know when we are whole. When we lose parts of ourselves, the integrity of our body is called into question. Along with the physical loss or damage to a part of our body, are the potentially related psychological and social losses:

- loss of expectation
- loss of role
- loss of self-esteem
- loss of self-confidence
- loss of security
- loss of control
- loss of independence
- loss of freedom

Not all these losses will be experienced by everyone who experiences a loss of part of themselves. However, there are always associated psychological and social losses when our body is threatened.

As Maria McCarthy's story illustrates, her physical losses very much implicated psychological ones. The emotional and psychological reactions to the loss will depend on the significance of the bodily part. The removal of a leg will cause more distress than that of a tooth. A mastectomy produces profound effects because our Western world idealises breasts which symbolise a woman's sexuality.

Individuals vary widely in their reactions to loss of body or bodily function. A whole range of psychological factors also play a part: how the individual views the part involved means that arthritis disfiguring fingers and hands might have one meaning and a leg amputation quite another meaning. The individual's reactions are further affected by what links there are between these losses and past losses and how the individual learned to come to terms with their previous losses over a lifetime.

The extent of the potential loss for a nation is clear, when we consider the fact that there are many millions of operations every year and all of these have the potential to produce grief reactions. These grief reactions are not confined to the person who experiences the loss directly. These grief reactions reach much further into the family and support network of the person who loses part of themselves.

Dr Castelnuovo-Tedesco, Vanderbilt University Professor of Psychiatry sums up the challenge of physical loss: *'All of us would like to feel we are somehow capable of stemming the tide of aging, accidents and all sorts of dire events which can overtake us – and finally and ultimately the death of the organism which represents the full obliteration of the self. Losses of parts of the body as well as the losses of other people remind us of our own mortality and our own vulnerability – questions which are difficult for anyone to think about it any clear or protracted kind of way. But the issue essentially contains some or all of these questions.'*

THE IMPACT OF ILLNESS, ACCIDENT AND IMPAIRMENT

For Maria McCarthy, her accident and her physical losses meant not only dealing with broken bones and years of rehabilitation, but also the psychological effects of such severe physical injuries. A physical loss means a loss of expectations – our hopes and plans are shattered, maybe temporarily, possibly permanently.

We all have plans. Some of us even start each day with a plan or timetable for the day's events. Often, we are annoyed if our plans have to be changed, but rarely do such changes cause deep emotional distress. Even those of us who make New Year resolutions are not certain of the eventual outcome. Yet, when things don't work out as we expected, we have a sense of sadness and feelings of being let-down. It's fair to say that, unconsciously, most of us expect to live normal, healthy lives, and a physical set-back is very confronting. How difficult it must be for a young adult in the prime of their life to become a paraplegic or quadriplegic after an accident. How difficult is must be for the healthy mid-life person suddenly to develop worrying symptoms that are diagnosed as multiple sclerosis. When our physical health is threatened in such ways, we have to learn new skills and to adapt and recover through grief-work.

Every year, millions of people suffer a first stroke. Although widely perceived to be an affliction of old age, around 10% of strokes occur in people under 55. A third of all stroke victims make a good, although almost never full, recovery, a third are left with permanent disability and a third die. Most strokes are caused by a weakness in the wall of the blood vessel in the brain. Strokes that damage the right hemisphere of the brain cause physical disability on the left-hand side of the body. Damage to the left hemisphere can cause paralysis on the right-hand side of the body and can lead to problems with speech and language called aphasia.

At the age of 42, Robert McCrum, a novelist and editor-in-chief at Faber and Faber, suffered a stroke in his sleep which left him paralysed down his left side. Sarah Lyall, a journalist and his wife of 10 weeks, just happened to be out of the country on an assignment when Robert had the stroke. Sarah describes how she became more and more concerned, and then frantic, as the phone rang and she left increasingly desperate voice-mail messages. Finally, Robert managed to roll himself onto the floor and began the tortuous journey downstairs to the phone. He drifted in and out of consciousness and finally managed to ring his mother. Robert's mother told Sarah:

'He's collapsed. He can't move.' Sarah had replied, 'I'll call him' and was told, 'I don't think you should'. It was at that point that Sarah packed her bags to get on the next plane back to London.

Robert has written a book about his experience, ***My year off: rediscovering life after a stroke***. He writes,

> 'I had to face up to the slow process of recovery, which, in the case of a stroke, offers a moving target: one is imperceptibly getting better. I had also to learn to adjust, and to wait. Before all this, I could slip across the street to post a letter in the time it takes to type a sentence. For about a year, I had to raise myself from my chair, find my walking stick, limp to the front door (say, 3 minutes), negotiate the steps to the street, and make my way to the corner (roughly 5 minutes), and then hobble back and collapse on the sofa, as though I had just run a marathon. I used to be known for the impressionistic speed with which I could do things, but I have now become friends with slowness, both as a concept and as a way of life. Sometimes it is difficult to admit that the stroke was an irrevocable event in my personal history. To admit that I have been scared and lonely is as difficult as it is to admit that I can sometimes feel a profound anger toward the world that has done this to me.'

The anger and rage that people often feel is related to their sense of injustice, the 'why me?' question and frustration with the disability, their body failing them and their sense of lack of control.

Other physical losses which threaten to change a person's life are those of loss of a body part or bodily functioning. The grief related to our physical integrity being so challenged – our wholeness – can be very intense.

Imagine the grief of receiving a life-threatening diagnosis. Learning to live with a high level of uncertainty is stressful. The grief experienced and the adjustment that needs to be made to life can be enormous. Learning to trust your body again when it has betrayed you is very hard.

Breast cancer is an epidemic. Breast cancer is one of the diseases women fear most. One in nine women will develop breast cancer in her life.

Joyce Wadler, in her poignant and amusing book, ***My Breast: One Woman's Cancer Journey***, begins with the following words,

'I have a scar on my left breast, four inches long, which runs from the right side of my breast to just above the nipple. Nick, who I no longer see, once said if anyone asked, I should say I was attacked by a jealous woman. The true story, which I prefer, is that a surgeon made the cut, following a line I had drawn for him the night before. He had asked me where I wanted the scar, and I had put on a black strapless bra and my favorite party dress and drawn a line in ink just below the top of the bra, a good four inches below the tumor.'

Joyce Wadler describes how her denial and shock gave way to acceptance and determination. As she says, *'This is a modern story. Me and my cancer. I won.'*

We have all heard of women in their initial grief, after diagnosis, being immobilised by the word 'cancer'. It is a scary word. One woman, Jane, 52, says, *'People hear the word and think 'death'. It's like believing in pointing the bone. I've had two previous experiences with cancer and I won't give up. You have to stay positive.'* Another woman, Elsie, 43, had a busy schedule as a single, working mother and believed her task-oriented attitude saved her life. She responded to her feelings of grief by getting as much information as she could about cervical cancer. She says, *'I wanted to understand what was happening. It helped me to think I had some control. I knew something and I didn't feel helpless.'*

While it is important to maintain a positive attitude, these women also speak directly about how 'lousy' they felt – about themselves and their bodies. They lived with falling self-esteem, constrained in their choices in life, feeling out of control much of the time, had their hopes truly shaken and in some cases, lost their previous independence. When they were recovering from the effects of operations or debilitating treatments, they often had to rely on the actual physical and practical support of others.

LOSS OF EXPECTATIONS AND THE BURDEN OF GUILT

Loss of expectation for some people represents loss of control. Loss of expectations and the grieving that goes with it is a complex matter. Guilt is implicated when parents wonder whether it is the fault of one of them that a child has a problem at birth. This sort of speculation can lead to relationship disharmony and breakdown. There might be a strong belief in one parent that the disability must be someone's fault and that the fault lies with their partner. Statistical evidence shows the rate of relationship breakdown to be extremely high after the birth of a child with physical and or intellectual problems.

One couple came to counselling because they had engaged in years of continual speculation. They had become 'stuck' in their attempts to find an explanation for their son's autism, and their relationship was suffering. Over and over, they asked, 'Why?', 'Why is he like this?', 'What happened?' and then one or other, usually the woman, speculated, 'It must have been because of X' or 'During my pregnancy, I remember doing such and such and that must have...'

Four years after the birth of their son, this couple had not accepted their loss – they had delayed their grieving in their guilty search for explanations.

In a beautifully written piece, called **Becoming Deaf**, David Wright reconstructs his loss and his perception of that loss,

> 'It was my father, looking in on his way to the office.
>
> His visit inaugurated a ceremony which was to be observed every morning so long as I stayed at the nursing-home. Pulling his gold watch (it had rococo Victorian initials engraven on the back) from his waistcoat-pocket, he would hold it up to my ear.
>
> 'Can you hear the tick?' I would shake my head. My head was thick with bandages.
>
> My father never failed to pay his early morning visit or to administer the ritual of the watch. It gave me a first clue to the discovery I was to make in the course of the next few days: that I had completely lost my hearing.
>
> One would think that deafness must have been self-evident from the first. On the contrary it took me some time to find out what had happened. I had to deduce the fact of deafness through a process of reasoning. I did not notice it.

No one inhabits a world of total silence: I had 'heard' the doctor's car driving me to the hospital, while the tread of the nurse coming into my room used to wake me in the morning – how was I to know? Nobody told me.

It was made more difficult to perceive because from the very first my eyes had unconsciously begun to translate motion into sound. My mother spent most of the day beside me and I understood everything she said. Why not? Without knowing it I had been reading her mouth all my life. When she spoke I seemed to hear her voice. It was an illusion which persisted even after I knew it was an illusion. My father, my cousin, everyone I had known, retained phantasmal voices. That they were imaginary, the projections of habit and memory, did not come home to me until I had left hospital. One day I was talking with my cousin and he, in a moment of inspiration, covered his mouth with his hand as he spoke. Silence! Once and for all I understood that when I could not see I could not hear.

But that was later. Only little by little did I attain right knowledge of my condition. The watch business put me on the track. From discovering that there were some things I could not hear I progressed to the truth that I could hear nothing.

The discovery in no way upset me. It was very gradually that I understood what had happened. Then, being innocent of experience, I was spared –as my parents certainly were not spared – speculation or foresight of the ways in which the rest of my life might be modified and hampered. For my parents what had happened was a catastrophe; to me it was an incident. It seemed neither important nor extraordinary except in so far that everything seems important and extraordinary when one is seven. Like animals, children are able to accept injuries in a casual manner, with apparent courage.

Children have a resilience and adaptability that must seem unbelievable to an adult. No courage bore me up at the age of seven; nature or whatever you call the almost unthwartable energy of life which inhabits all young creatures – the drive to go on living under any circumstances – made deafness seem to me, at the time, one of the normal accidents of living.

In the case of a deaf child it is the parents who do the suffering, at least to begin with. Mine found themselves faced with all sorts of questions to which they had to find answers that might not, for all they knew, exist. How was I to be educated? How far would I be able to lead a 'normal' life? When I grew up, would I be capable of ordinary social intercourse? How would I earn a living? You can imagine what forebodings weighed on them. They could not know that things might work out better than they feared.

PROMPT FOR YOUR PEN

Exercise   **Reflection on David Wright's story**

Reflection on David Wright's reconstruction of his discovery of deafness.

Earlier it was suggested that children might be more adaptable because they are learning every day and not yet set in their assumptions of the world.

How does David Wright's story confirm this possibility?

What did you make of his reaction to his deafness?

What did you make of his parents' reaction?

What was important for you in his story?

THE GRIEFS OF DISABILITY

The spectrum of 'disability' ranges from complete dependency, as in a high-level spinal injury which results in almost total paralysis and a need for full-time care through difficulties in mobility, sight and hearing, which vary in their effects on the person's life to breathlessness, which may cause major problems or may be relatively minor in everyday living. Both genetic and acquired disabilities have components of loss of expectations.

It's been found that when a child with an impairment is born or when a person acquires a disability as a result of accident or illness, a lot of the initial grief manifests itself as anger.

People who are born with a disability sometimes show anger towards parents for being over-protective, or in very rare cases, under-protective. There often is anger towards society for failure to validate the disabled, recognise their disability by providing appropriate facilities or because of perceived stigma.

With both genetic and acquired disability, there is frustration and anger, usually directed against the disability itself, but often, displaced onto people, mostly those closest to the person. Sometimes, these supporters and carers feel frustrated and angry as well – with the disability and with the person. Often, people are frightened by the apparent irrationality and strength of their anger.

Sarah Lyall and Robert McCrum speak candidly in an article in **Woman's Journal**, about the anger they both felt:

Sarah says, *'It was very hard for me because he'd been so competent. He could really handle anything. I'd been out with someone a few years before who was just such a child and depended on me for everything. I really liked Robert's independence, and all of a sudden he was helpless. Even when he came home after three months and could walk a little, he couldn't carry anything, he couldn't dress himself. All those domestic things which I had been so happy to share were left totally to me... I never yelled at you, but I would cry a lot.'*

Robert says, *'We had one or two little episodes, didn't we?'*

'But you felt angry, like me.'

'Yes', Robert agrees, *'I felt the same, I'd really rage at Sarah on occasions. I feel bad about it now, but there were one or two moments when I lost it completely. It was shameful really.'*

'No, it wasn't,' Sarah insists. *'I was actually really glad that you at least had an outlet for your frustration. If you were a woman, you wouldn't hesitate to say how bad you felt, whereas many men can't do that.'*

The themes of anger, frustration and crying return time and again in accounts of early grief-work. Loss of independence and the grief that it brings is central to the feelings of sadness and frustration.

Researchers have found that decremental downhill progress appears to make people more vulnerable to getting stuck in their grief-work and developing a depression, more so than a disability which remains stable. Multiple sclerosis, Parkinson's disease, Huntington's disease, motor neurone disease, muscular dystrophies and Alzheimer's present a greater challenge to the person and their family in their attempt to reach resolution. Certain other conditions can present as encroaching disability, for example, vascular disease, rheumatoid arthritis, cancer and a series of small 'strokes' all create continuing disability. Each condition has its own pattern and set of expectations. Each condition brings with it a prolonged period of loss and grief for the sufferer and their family and friends.

If it is possible to speak of advantages, then we might say that chronic disability and prolonged illness, in theory, give the patient and family a chance to talk about how they feel. Most people find this difficult to do without some professional assistance.

LOSSES OF THE PSYCHE

Our psychological health is critical to our feeling of well-being. Our psychological health helps to define our sense of place in the world. Our self-image is of extreme importance to us. If our self-image is strong, then we can lead happy and fulfilling lives. We perceive ourselves as worthwhile human beings. Loss of self-esteem is linked to other psychological losses such as, loss of self-confidence, loss of control, loss of independence, loss of freedom and loss of choice.

CHALLENGES TO OUR SELF-ESTEEM

Our self-esteem can be challenged at any age. The pre-school child is lowered in his own esteem when he continually is pushed out of games by other children. The school child may feel rejected and lose esteem in their own eyes and others when they are not selected for ball game teams. Adolescent girls, in particular, will suffer loss of self-esteem if they are excluded from whispered secrets and the intimacy of cliques. As a young adult, a person will experience loss of self-esteem when he fails to get the job he wants or to get a place at university in the course he has dreamed about since boyhood.

Loss of parental and family self-esteem is felt when teenage and adult children are found to be substance-dependent, mentally ill, or to be involved in criminal activities. There are parents who experience feelings of grief, loss and guilt when their children's lives do not reflect cherished parental values. For example, if educational achievement, traditional marriage and religious observance are important as the foundation of a happy life, the likely response by parents to the flouting of these values might be: 'Where did we go wrong?', 'What should we have done that we didn't do?' The parents experience loss of self-esteem as a consequence.

The elderly person loses self-esteem in today's rapid, technological world when they cannot understand the computer jargon of their children and grand-children, nor cope with the microwave, negotiate Automatic Teller Machine transactions, or cope with the speed of activity in the world around them.

These examples and many others all mean having to grieve the smaller or larger losses that our self-esteem and our sense of self have experienced. People who have been assaulted or violated in some way find that they grieve their drop in self-esteem and struggle to recover their self-image.

DAYS OF WEEPING

Susan, 24, who was raped and left tied up for eight hours before someone found her, begins her story with the words, *'I have lost the person I was going to be in my '30s.'* She continues by saying she was angry about her assault for many months and found her drop in self-esteem affected every aspect of her life. She continues,

*'For months I would have flashbacks to the rape and I'd
lock myself in my bedroom – I just wanted to be alone.
One night, I felt so bad, totally worthless, so I locked myself
in the bathroom and cut myself. My mother panicked and
called my boyfriend, who broke down the door. I couldn't
have sex with my boyfriend for three months, I felt so dirty.*

*And I would cry and cry so much I thought I'd get on my mother
and sister's nerves.*

*With my boyfriend I felt so guilty, because I
couldn't help hurting him. I'd snap his head off
sometimes, I just had all this anger in me and I
needed to let it out. He stuck with me and with his
help and my family's help, I've made small steps forward.
But I still feel I've lost who I was. I'm not the same person.'*

This sense of having lost a part of your old self and not being the same person is true in many cases of another sort of violation, when a woman has an abortion. Women have abortions for many different reasons. Although it is easy to judge and say, 'Well, she chose to have an abortion', the reality is always more complex. Abortion is an unrecognised loss and means silent grieving. The psychological consequences are often traumatic and sometimes, the grief remains unresolved.

Clare, 54, suffered from chronic depression most of her life, with low self-esteem and confidence. By the time Clare was in the '30s she was alcohol dependent and often physically unwell. She had had numerous hospitalisations but had not confronted her 'real' loss until she was in her 50s. A breakthrough in counselling allowed her to face herself and her loss for the first time in decades. She had an abortion at 19, when as a university student, she knew she was in no position to become a mother. Her Catholic upbringing and the secrecy surrounding the abortion left a legacy of guilt, plummeting self-esteem and confidence and 'days of weeping' which continued for nearly 30 years.

She says,

'I've paid a huge price for that abortion. I have had to live with my loss for decades. I have had to live with myself for decades. It has been hard to accept what I did. Some days I still think it was an unforgiveable act. But I know that's irrational thinking. I lost the chance to be a mother. I have never been able to face myself about that until just recently. I felt very badly about being a woman for years – well, for most of my life.'

For many women, an abortion, even if freely 'chosen' can seem like a violation. Violations of other sorts can also leave a mark on the psyche. These marks can be difficult to erase, as grief-work required to do so can seem overwhelming.

CAPTURE AND CAPTIVITY

Professor Zahava Solomon has researched and theorised about the effects of capture and captivity on prisoners of war (POW). The losses of captivity are numerous and include:

- death of commanders and comrades
- bodily losses of limbs, sense of function
- freedom
- social contact, social support and social roles
- autonomy
- hopes, dreams and ideas
- essential parts of former identity
- dignity and self-esteem

The possible range of physical, psychological and social losses that a POW can suffer are staggering. The grief enormous. Yet the conditions of captivity do not allow for grief-work to be performed readily nor for easy resolution of that grief.

The most obvious losses are the tangible ones of limbs, sense and functioning stemming from physical injury. Death, disappearance and injury to comrades and commanders, these losses of battle can be seen and processed – in time. However, the intangible losses are no less real. Capture and captivity subject the POW to more losses, some of these amplifications of battlefield losses, some derived from the nature and meaning of being taken and held a prisoner of war. According to Professor Solomon, *'Captivity is designed to destroy the victim's sense of self in relation to others and prolonged and repeated traumatic exposure damages crucial elements of the individual's self structure.'* Other researchers have found that people have reported such alterations in themselves as a result of incarceration in concentration camps. Some people have described themselves as being another person. Others felt that they were not a person at all.

The POW, on his return home, will have an enormous task to complete his grieving. Oral and written accounts often give a picture of the power of individual differences. Some people will adjust to their traumatic conditions a little better and begin some grieving for their multiple losses. Others will carry the wound to their psyche back home. It may stay with them for years, often decades to come. Much of the depression seen in returned soldiers and POW is related to their unresolved grief.

One of the biggest challenges for the returned soldier and POW is to re-engage in society at home. One Vietnam soldier described this feeling as 'unreal'. He said, *'One minute you're in a jungle fighting a war, and the next, you're back at home in the suburbs. It didn't feel real.'*

This expectation that people involved in the horrors of war return home and resume a former identity without the need for recognition, validation and psychological assistance is now outdated. Services now exist to help those who have suffered trauma, losses and need to grieve. The very real need for counselling services is evidenced by the fact that some returned soldiers from Vietnam are only receiving help many years after their return, or indeed, still need counselling after all these years. Psychologically and socially, the losses sustained by these people need to be resolved.

OUR SOCIAL LOSSES

There are many social losses that can visit a person in their life-time. Retirement, saying good-bye to your working life represents a loss of status for many people. It also represents losses of other kinds.

OUT OF WORK

No number of seminars on retirement, preparing people for financial security will inoculate them from the often unbearable shocks of retirement. Unless the person is prepared to develop and alter, they face an empty daily round of doing nothing, or the merry-go-round of sports and/or games.

Loss of role is part of the cultural shock of retirement. For some, there is also a marked loss of expectation because their expectations have been based on an unreal picture of retirement. Alternatively, the shining future they had imagined has been interrupted by unexpected illness. This illness might have destroyed the dreams of the Golden Years.

In the case of loss of employment, of retrenchment, where the job loss is unexpected and usually, unwanted, the negative effect on the person's self-esteem may be tremendous. This crisis might stir up all the losses a person ever failed to work out in their life-time. If the loss is not accepted at an unconscious level, then depression can set in, and the grief remains unresolved until the person accepts the loss as a reality.

In our fast-moving, high-tech world, job loss has become common and people who have lost their jobs and livelihood almost overnight have commented on the ruthlessness of the process – and the assault on their self-esteem. If the person has options for work, then the grieving process might be short and a new job will help assuage their sense of loss. However, if the person is 50 plus and has few or no options for another job, then the blow to his or her sense of self will be great.

Complicating any possible grieving will be other social factors. These include whether the person is the sole breadwinner in the family or whether they have debts that can't be met without full-time employment and whether there are any other physical or psychological concerns in other members of the family.

WHEN YOU CAN'T HAVE A BABY

Infertility is a personal loss at both the psychological and social level. Our society continues to expect women to fulfil 'Nature's' role for them. Although it has been suggested that more and more women are choosing to remain childless, there are still pressures, particularly on married women, to reproduce.

Women who have made both 'natural' and assisted reproductive technology attempts and not succeeded in having a baby must grieve this loss. They must grieve all the babies they will never have. Their loss continues to be a silent one, despite its obvious social dimension: grieving the loss of expectation of motherhood.

GRIEFS OF MIGRATION

Migration represents a loss at the personal, social and cultural levels. Change, loss, grief, more change and potential growth are all part of the process of migration and resettlement. Many migrants speak about the trauma, about being 'shell-shocked' for a period of time after arrival. They speak of great personal losses, psychological pressures and personal hardships. J. William Worden's typology of symptoms of grief experience can readily be applied to many of the stories told by migrants.

George, a man now in his 70s, was called Gyuri, but people found it too hard to say, so he Anglicised it. He arrived in Australia in 1956 and he says,

'Nothing in life is as you imagine it to be. When I arrived I thought Sydney was such an ugly, modern city. I missed the beauty of Budapest. I missed a lot of things. In the hostel in Austria I imagined Sydney to be a Garden of Eden. I was very disappointed when I arrived. I felt numb for a long time. It took a long time for me to adjust. The early years for me were very hard. They were hard physically and psychologically.'

Migrants not only speak of emotional aspects of loss and readjustment, but also physical sensations that are likened to grief. George continues,

'In the early days, it was like I was in a movie. Nothing was real. I was watching another man do what I was doing. And I felt sick a lot of the time....and tired, always.'

The sense of depersonalisation and lack of energy are sensations shared in common with grieving people. So are the physical symptoms of getting ill, being unable to sleep well and constant tiredness.

Many migrants report that they begin their grief-work by banding together and processing their experience together, to grieve the past and make sense of the present. Collective and individual responses to dealing with their sense of loss are important for migrants in their grief-work. Setting up cultural networks to maintain a sense of identity, meeting in formal groups and informal gatherings can provide the security of knowing they can redefine themselves without losing everything from their past.

Connecting with compatriots and talking about old times, the difficulties encountered in their new life and their hopes for the future can offer migrants the opportunity of ventilating their thoughts and feelings – and understanding they are not alone in their sense of loss, nor their resettlement challenges.

In the play, **Hungarian Sunday**, by Barbara Altoraji-Albury, one character shares with the others how migrants recreated some aspects of European culture and atmosphere by patronising the early Sydney cafes,

Rudi:	In the fifties, you couldn't get real coffee.
Joe:	And then came Repins in George Street.
Olga:	And in the Piccadilly Arcade.
Rudi:	The Europa.
Joe:	Very chic.
Joe:	But in the Piccadilly Arcade, we could imagine we were in a Budapest coffee shop before the war. You could order a short black or a milk coffee, or if you were feeling a little decadent, a Vienna – a black coffee with a swirl of cream on top.

So, as these words suggest, by recreating a piece of the past – something familiar, people could cope better with the losses and the challenges. Other strategies in their grief-work involved writing letters home, speaking about 'home' and the 'motherland' with fellow migrants and the process of story-telling in their families. These were important ways of finding coherence and meaning which act to offset the feelings of grief and dispossession.

OUR CULTURAL LOSSES

Most of us experience a number of cultural losses in our lives. Many of these will not necessarily cause great distress, however, they need to be acknowledged. Whenever we experience social network changes, because of changes in our environment, we have the potential grief of cultural loss. Spiritual changes herald a cultural loss – whenever we are challenged in our spiritual beliefs or change our spiritual affiliation we need to grieve the loss. Migration, of course is a good example of cultural loss.

Cultural losses also relate to the circles in which we move. In working with drug and alcohol dependent people, it is often confronting when a person, motivated to change their destructive behaviour, talks about the great sense of grief in leaving behind some of the security and comforts of their small cultural network. One heroin dependent young woman told me, *'It's not only the heroin I'm leaving behind, but all my friends – it's a hard thing to do. I've known people to give up – and then return, because they've missed their friends – you know, the whole scene.'*

The interconnectedness of physical, psychological, social and cultural losses is often very clear. Very rarely is a physical loss uncomplicated by a number of psychological losses. Similarly, a social loss has psychological components and possibly cultural dimensions as well.

PROMPT FOR YOUR PEN

Exercise **Nominating your types of losses**

Earlier, you were asked to do a similar exercise. Now that you have more information and you have reflected on your own life experiences, answer the following questions:

• Have you ever experienced one sort of loss and found there were other types of loss within it?
• What was your initial reaction?
• What did you learn from the experience?

6

LOSING IMPORTANT PEOPLE

Nothing on earth can make up for the loss
of one who has loved you.

SELMA LAGERLOF [Jerusalem, 1915]

Whether through separation, divorce or death, losing important people means a loss of significant proportions. It means change, adjustment and learning to live differently. The relationship you had with that important person in your life is either no longer, or no longer the same. Dealing with the loss of attachment is part of your good grief-work.

Grief is a personal reaction. However, because we do not live in a vacuum, we are influenced by the groups and society in which we live. Our view, to some extent, is informed and influenced by the attitudes and value systems of society. These views, attitudes and value systems change over time.

DEALING WITH
SEPARATION AND DIVORCE

In the latter part of the twentieth century, societal attitudes to separation and divorce have changed dramatically. Perhaps even more dramatic have been the shifts in perception of various religious institutions regarding separation and divorce. These changes and shifts have meant that divorced couples and their children are not as stigmatised as they once were. Generally speaking, there is more tolerance for 'broken families' and 'single parent families' and less blaming and vilification of family members who have decided not to live together anymore. Nevertheless, some people still might feel a little stigmatised.

When a major relationship breaks down people often analyse endlessly 'what went wrong'. The end of a relationship usually provokes strong passions and people want to find answers, to help them understand. It's not difficult to understand this passion and analysis when we consider that we invest so much emotional energy in our major relationship. We also hold tremendous expectations for this relationship – often unrealistic expectations. When we enter the relationship, we believe we want our partner to provide us with everything: emotional support, absolute trust, unconditional love, wonderful sex and great companionship. When these expectations are not met and the relationship fails, the 'death' of the ideal relationship we so cherished is painful to us and we feel aggrieved.

These dreams and expectations and their fit or otherwise with reality are captured in Pope's poem, **_The Wife of Bath_**: _'They dream in courtship, but in wedlock wake.'_

The end of a relationship provokes the usual grief reactions, although people have different individual responses and healing times. Relationships can end with one partner leaving the other for a new person. The partner being left usually experiences considerable loss of self-esteem. This person may feel 'dumped' and resent the power their partner is asserting by leaving them. However, although the partner doing the leaving may not experience as dramatic a fall in self-esteem, they are unlikely to emerge with their self-esteem totally intact. Separation always brings deep passions into play – and the partner leaving might experience pangs of guilt. Sometimes, the partner being left compromises her or his self-esteem further by bargaining with the departing partner. She or he might promise to do anything to keep the partner, promises to change, to go to couples counselling and other uncharacteristic promises. Very often, this bargaining does not work, as the departing partner has emotionally disengaged from the relationship. In effect, some people 'leave' or separate from their partners long before they ever give notice of their departure.

The grief of separation and divorce involves:

- loss of self-esteem
- loss of security
- loss of self-confidence
- loss of role
- loss of expectations

Very often, there is intense loneliness which follows separation and divorce. Many people have reported that individuals whom they considered good friends seemingly 'dropped' them overnight. This phenomenon seems to be related to fear by others that they might 'get involved' or be affected emotionally by proxy, perhaps even contaminated by the misfortune of the divorcing couple or person. Some women have spoken angrily and others in surprised tones by what they perceive to be the fear of their sexuality. These women have said they are convinced that other women believe that, now they are single again, they will adopt a predatory approach in looking for a new lover.

One such woman is Fiona, 44, whose marriage of 20 years came to an end – as did her friendship with a woman whom she considered her best friend. At first Fiona was surprised, then hurt, and finally she became angry at the assumption that she was 'after' her friend's husband. She says,

'I still can't believe Diane thought I would go after her husband. I mean it's not like he is an oil painting. He's a lovely man, but not my type – and I thought she knew that. I thought she knew my taste in men. We often shared confidences about what we fancied in a man, what drove us mad – you know, girl talk – so I was shocked when she dropped me. She was subtle at first, but as the weeks passed she became more direct and then I got angry. We had

*quite a scene. It was something I could have done without. I was counting on
her support and all I got was her rejection. It shakes your trust when
something like this happens.'*

What baffled Fiona the most was that her friend had such little empathy
and couldn't understand that following hard on her husband's rejection,
Fiona needed compassion and understanding. Fiona was hurt and angry
about Diane's assumption of competition. Fiona felt misunderstood.

Fiona ended up having to deal with double grief. She had lost a husband
and a friend.

Fiona is not the only person who has experienced this combination of
loneliness resulting from the end of her marriage compounded by loss of
other significant social relationships.

Loss of the social relationships embedded in the extended family of
in-laws and other family connections can also be a source of grief. Many
people have good relationships with their partner's family and in the event
of separation, there are issues of loyalty and guilt that can confound these
otherwise positive relationships. If relationships are maintained with
grandparents only because 'of the children' then this can become a source
of further tension. The losses associated with changes in the family structure
can also lead to strained relationships between people who respect or even
like one another.

Another significant loss relates to the family celebrations which are
changed by separation and divorce. There are birthdays, anniversaries,
annual social events, picnics and vacations which the family 'always did'
together. Every family that has experienced separation has its unique set of
lost and changed events. One woman told me that she missed watching
'family' shows with her whole family. She felt sad whenever such a show
was on television and in the early months of separation, she could not bring
herself to watch these shows with her two daughters. It became such a
painful reminder of the 'lost' family life.

Of course, for some families, there will be benefits from separation and
divorce. Where there has been long-term stress, violence and ambivalence,

making a decision to separate can in itself bring relief. However, even under these circumstances, there are likely to be some regrets, a measure of guilt and possibly even depression. Even under such adverse circumstances, the couple will feel some loss of expectation of their relationship.

SEPARATION, DIVORCE AND THE 'BROKEN HEART'

Most people can empathise with someone whose partner has died. But in the case of separation and divorce, there are not customs or rites by which we recognise the death of the relationship and we have no ritualistic way to grieve over a divorce. For some people, separation and divorce becomes a 'living death' in so far as there is no way to prevent denial of end of the relationship.

For Jason, the actual divorce represented a death. Jason, 29, was distraught when his wife said she was leaving him because she was bored. Four years earlier, Liesel had told Jason that she found his stability very 'grounding'. He had been drawn by her energy and enthusiasm. It was ironic that for Liesel, the very quality that initially attracted her, become tiresome and made Jason uninteresting in her eyes, only four years later.

Liesel's comments and her leaving him were described by Jason as a 'body blow'. He suffered a loss in self-esteem, became withdrawn and depressed. He came to counselling sporadically for two years. He vacillated between wanting to work on his grief, and not wanting to let go of the past. This dilemma was encapsulated in his comment:

'My divorce came through last week. It's like a death after a long illness. Unless you've been there, it's hard to explain. I feel relief but, I feel it's still a tragedy.'

It was Jason's ability to finally verbalise his dilemma that ironically provided the opportunity for exploring further the work he needed to do to heal his heart.

Everyday language abounds in expressions such as 'He left her broken-hearted' or 'She broke his heart' or 'I was heart-broken when he left me'. We all are familiar with the metaphor of a 'broken heart' – of the person who has been left by their partner.

Barry, 39 found himself bargaining with his wife, Pat, when she told him she was leaving him for a colleague – someone whom Barry knew well. He says,

'I did everything I could to keep her. I lowered myself to promising anything, I even went so far as to agree to going to counselling with her – and she knew I hated that idea. She'd been trying to get me to go for years. I guess I didn't see it coming – until it hit me. But by then, all the promises were too late. What really depresses me when I think about it is how I demeaned myself, but at the time, I was desperate to hang on to her.'

Barry went on to reveal that he was angry with her for months. Then he felt guilty. He felt guilty because Pat had always wanted children and he had resisted the idea. He wondered if maybe she might have stayed had he agreed to a family. Barry continues,

'It took me ages to get over the blow – the grief – I got stuck in the angry phase and then all the guilt engulfed me. I think Pat was probably laughing – and I don't blame her – when she found out that I went to see a counsellor. I couldn't sort it out by myself. In the end, it was okay. But it was hell for a long time.'

Some people find that they 'get stuck', like Barry, in a particular phase and that they find it difficult to move on in their good grief work. At some level, Barry had a 'broken heart' – and his broken-heartedness manifested itself in becoming immobilised.

Anne, 35, was shocked when her relationship of three years ended. She and her boyfriend Darren, had spoken about marriage and they had been living together for eighteen months. She said,

'You don't think it's going to happen to you. And then it does. It comes as such a shock. I felt heart-broken. I loved him so much. He was everything to me. Even when I learnt that he had cheated on me, I wanted to keep going with the relationship. All my friends thought I was crazy. They'd say, "Look, he broke your heart – he's a bastard – he's not worth it. Forget him.' But I couldn't. Not for a long time. I couldn't let go. I went into therapy for a year to get over him.'

This idea of separation leading to a broken heart sounds very much like people understand – however subliminally – that separation means loss and results in grief. Anne spoke specifically of being heart-broken and having to go into therapy to piece herself together again. In her case, there appeared to be little anger, and more yearning.

Shakespeare, in a whimsical poem, **Sigh No More**, gives advice to Ladies who might sigh and cry:

Sigh no more Ladies, sigh no more
Men were deceivers ever,
One foote in Sea, and one on shore,
To one thing constant never,
Then sigh not so, but let them goe,
And be you blithe and bonnie,
Converting all your sounds of woe,
Into hey nony nony.

Sigh no more ditties, sing no moe,
Of dumps so dull and heavy,
The fraud of men was ever so,
Since summer first was leavy,
Then sigh not so, but let them goe,
And be you blithe and bonnie,
Converting all your sounds of woe,
Into hey nony nony.

But, for some people, feeling heart-broken leads to feelings of anger, vengeance and blaming.

Partners need to acknowledge that apportioning blame is not a productive exercise. In fact, indulging in blaming, name-calling and vilification can lead to grief going wrong. By continuing to blame and vilify, a person demonstrates their difficulty in accepting the loss of attachment – they are showing how they need to hang onto that attachment. Remember that the first task of grieving is to accept the reality of the loss. By continuing to talk about how your partner let you down, was at fault or is a nasty human being, a person might sound aggrieved, but they are not doing their grief-work. In fact, they are actively resisting that work and showing how much they need to remain attached. Their grief-work starts when they accept the loss and begin to feel and express their hurt feelings and their confusion, fear, loneliness and ambivalence.

CHILDREN AND THEIR REACTIONS

Many children experience divorce. Divorce is the fate of up to a third of Western marriage. Children, in particular, need to feel that it is not their fault that parents can no longer live together. It is important to reassure them. It is important that they hear that although Mum and Dad no longer feel the same way about each other as they did once, they still love the child. Children may feel guilty about their feelings towards their parents, and torn by divided loyalties. Some my secretly yearn – or even plot and plan to bring their parents together again. For some adolescents, separation and divorce may raise concerns about their own future relationships. Some adolescents may be relieved that their parents are no longer together to argue and hurt one another. Others may be angry and morally outraged by the behaviour of one or both parents.

Children too will experience intense grief and anxiety around the separation and divorce. It is important to remember that children's grief can take a different form at times – misbehaviour at school, withdrawing from school work or leisure activity and often along with a 'tuning out' also an 'acting out' of uncharacteristically aggressive behaviour. Sometimes, young children can get stuck in the early 'bargaining' stage by telling themselves that if they are good and well behaved then everything will be alright and their parents will stay together. Often children stay numb for a long time, refusing to speak – or even think – about the separation. Many adolescents react with anger. This anger is often related to the perceived disruption of their lives, at a critical time in their social and psychological development. Other teenagers have expressed relief that the marriage is over – but then add, angrily that they wished it had ended sooner.

Emma, 15, an 'acting-out' teenager indeed was acting out demonstrably her angry feelings about her parents' separation when she told her mother that she was taking drugs and couldn't care if she lived or died. This alarmed her mother, Peta, a reasonable woman, who had been worn out by the battle in the divorce courts with her former husband. Peta said,

'I hadn't realised how much things had affected Emma. She had always been such a sensible child so I thought she might cope quite well with the separation and then all that mess during the divorce. But I guess I was wishful thinking – I was so low in reserves myself that I didn't have the energy to give as much to her as I now realise she needed – and deserved. I was alarmed when she told me what she was up to. It was almost like she was challenging me to do something – to recognise her pain. I felt very guilty. I felt doubly guilty actually.'

Peta's comments tell us how she inadvertently neglected the needs of her daughter, because her own needs were so demanding. This is not an uncommon scenario. The adult is distressed, overwhelmed, exhausted, ambivalent, confused and angry and paying attention to their own emotions can absorb them. There is little energy, time or inclination left to pay attention to another's needs. This is not to suggest that parents don't care, but simply that when they find they have to pick up the pieces of their lives, their emotional reserves are so low that helping their child or children pick up the pieces of their lives might be too much to deal with.

Some young children, between the ages of three and five might regress and behave like much younger children. They might be confused and fearing abandonment by both parents. They might demand attention and display angry outbursts. This can be very alarming for parents.

Darien described what happened when her husband left her and children, Joanne, aged 10, Damien, aged 7 and Hannah, aged 4. The two older children were affected by his abrupt departure, but it was Hannah who concerned her mother most. Darien said,

'Hannah had always been a quiet child. She was toilet-trained and very good in every way. When my husband left, she began wetting and soiling herself and clinging to me like a frightened little animal. She was difficult at bedtime, crying and screaming for me until I finally got her off to sleep. She had to have a night- light on and if she woke at night, she would cry out and I'd have to go to her. I can't tell you what a change her father leaving us had on her. It was shocking to see the difference. It was such a dramatic 'before-and-after' situation. From a settled, good child, Hannah became a tantruming, irritable little girl.'

Darien heard that there was a children's grief support group not far from her home and she decided that Hannah would benefit. As it happened, Hannah did benefit. Through play and art-work, Hannah began to express her grief. A grief she was unable to express verbally.

How children will respond is a very individual matter. It will depend on their stage of development, their personality and what they have learned from role-models in their lives, including their parents. The context in which the separation and divorce take place is also an important factor in determining how a child will respond.

SEEKING HELP

It is at these critical times, when emotional reserves are low and people need nurturing that professional help and support groups are helpful.

Sometimes young children have a very black and white view of the world. They believe that someone must be to blame for the bad things that have happened. As noted earlier, often children will blame themselves. Sometimes, an angry parent will turn a child against the other parent. This is unreasonable and damaging to the child's sense of well-being.

In one study, researchers found that up to 80% of parents either didn't explain to their pre-school children what was happening or gave them an explanation that the children couldn't understand, nor deal with.

As one counsellor put it, *'Somebody has to explain to parents how to explain things to children.'*

Seeking professional help for you and your child or children is not shameful. It might prove to be the buoyant life raft you all need in a turbulent emotional sea.

You need to be provided with adequate support to help express the feelings that confront you and must be worked through: guilt, fear, anxiety, loneliness and confusion.

DOING SOME REFLECTION

A separation and divorce closes one door. However, you might know the old adage: 'When one door closes, another opens.' At first, you might dismiss this saying as trite, but, at its essence, it offers you the idea of welcoming new opportunities.

In the aftermath of a separation or divorce, you might have the opportunity of discovering new strength, interests and hopes and dreams to guide your choices in the future. It is important to get in touch with new choices and possibilities.

PROMPT FOR YOUR PEN

Exercise	Discovering new opportunities

• Make a list of all the things you find fun, that give you pleasure.
• Think of two friends who might be interested in doing some of these activities with you.

As you enter this new phase of your life, think of people who are part of your support system. Make a list of their name and beside each name write how they might offer you support.
For example who might be interested in doing new things with you?
Who can listen to you empathically and sit with your doubts about the future?
Who can affirm your new efforts?
Who can cheer you up when the going gets tough?

GRIEVING OVER DEATH

Historical changes over the last century have meant that people today are less familiar with death. In earlier times, people died at home with their family around them. This meant that family members experienced death at first hand and considered it a natural event. It has been said that increasingly, we are living in a death-defying, death-denying society, and it is not uncommon to find people in their forties and fifties who have not had close personal experiences of death. Today, the majority of deaths occur in hospitals or other institutions. Funeral directors, so much part of the process now, did not exist a century ago. Much of their function today belonged to the family in days gone by.

It is true to say that societal attitudes and beliefs have become more secular, although it is still the case that religion and faith play a large part in many people's attitudes and beliefs around death.

EXAMINING OUR ATTITUDES TO LIFE, DEATH AND DYING

In the following adapted excerpt by Peter Cotton, Sir Mark Oliphant reflects on his work, life and death. Read the passage and reflect yourself on the main features you gleaned from the piece.

Presence of mind

Sir Mark Oliphant was once a giant of Australian science. He was a key player in the development of the atomic bomb during World War II and led a team of scientists which gave the Allies airborne radar. At 92, Sir Mark says he's now ready to die.

He spends his days writing letters to friends and working on a piece he's called 'Nunc Demitis'. It's his last major work. The Latin title is drawn from a phrase in the Bible's Song of Simeon which translates, 'Lord, let now thy servant depart in peace'. There's urgency in his efforts. He says his intellect is fading faster than his body. He won't publish 'Nunc Demitis'; he'll give copies to a few friends.

'I have no feelings about death at all,' Oliphant says. 'I just hope it's quick and painless.'

Despite his focus on mortality, he is still mobile and basically independent. He lives in Canberra's Red Hill in a small unit dominated by a large study. Its walls are lined with books and mementos. There are photographs from his time as governor of South Australia – meetings with the famous and influential.

These days the man who had a major role in the modern understanding of nuclear physics doesn't like to talk about things nuclear. He abandoned that work immediately after the atomic bombs fell on Hiroshima and Nagasaki. His interests now focus on the health of the planet and its people. He says it might have been better had the Manhattan Project failed. But he admits that such a thought is unrealistic. 'Knowing how science works, one recognises that if we hadn't done it somebody else would have', he says.

That Mark Oliphant was in a position to have such a profound effect on the course of world history is a tribute to both his intellect and tenacity. Here is a son of the Adelaide working class who ascended to the world's science elite. Associates through his working life include some of the century's great scientific minds, people such as Einstein, Planck, Lawrence and Rutherford.

His pivotal role in the development of the atomic bomb, though, came by chance early in the war. Two scientists in his department at Cambridge University's prestigious Cavendish Laboratories, Rudolf Peierls and Otto Frisch, were German Jews. Designated enemy aliens and banned from working with Oliphant on his radar project, the two secreted themselves in a corner of the lab and came up with a ground-breaking proposal for a nuclear weapon using separated uranium 235.

Oliphant recognised great potential in the work of Peierls and Frisch. He gave his friend and colleague Ernest Lawrence a copy of the Germans' paper. Impressed, Lawrence became a prime sponsor of the subsequent Manhattan Project. The research carried out by Peierls and Frisch in Oliphant's laboratory was a key to the production of the world's first atomic bomb.

Oliphant plays down his part in getting the project up and running: 'It's just luck that puts you in particular position at a particular time,' he says.

Now, almost 50 years after the blasts that decimated Hiroshima and Nagasaki, Oliphant dismisses the nuclear conflagration scenarios that have dominated the modern psyche. He's a believer in mankind's will to survive. Any hostile use of nuclear weapons, he says, will be limited and local.

He sees the population bomb as a far greater threat. 'I think in the end man will be forced to preserve the ecology of the earth so it can support a reasonable population in a decent way.'

'There is always a chance for retrieval. In general I'm an optimist, but only if we take certain precautions, like limiting population growth, preserving the fertility of the earth and implementing conservation measures.'

Though the title of his last written work comes from the Bible, Oliphant draws no comfort from religion in the face of death. 'It's goodbye,' he says, 'Nobody's ever been able to describe an afterlife except in ridiculous terms. People sitting on either side of God playing harps and singing,' he chuckles.

'No, I don't believe in heaven or hell,' he says. 'But one might always be surprised.'

Adapted from the Good Weekend: 6 August, 1994

Postscript: Sir Mark was born in 1901 and died in 2000. He was eulogised for his sensitivity to the human condition and his passion for the environment.

PROMPT FOR YOUR PEN

Exercise   Exploring your own attitudes

- How would you describe Sir Mark Oliphant's attitude to death?

- Think back to a situation in which you heard some one or some people talking about death. What words did they use? Were they open about the topic?

- How would you describe your attitude to death? What words do you use when referring to death and dying?

If you are to do your good grief-work successfully, then you must have a reasonable level of awareness about your thoughts and feelings on the matter of death.

DEATH IN ALL ITS FORMS

There are four major categories of death:

- natural death: either expected or sudden
- accidental death
- suicide
- murder

Each of these forms of death can provoke a different level of intensity when it comes to grief. Some of these forms of death may appear more 'normal' than others. This perception of 'normality' or otherwise, may affect the grief process. For instance, the death of a much loved grandparent after a long illness may cause great distress and sadness, but it does not seem as contrary to the natural order of life as the death of a young child. The death of a grandparent who has lived a long and full life may be perceived as more 'normal' than the death of a young child, who would 'normally' be expected to not die before his parents.

In terms of perceived 'normality', a violent death may be harder to accept, whatever the age of the deceased, than that of a 98-year-old who dies quietly in her sleep.

GRIEVING OVER A NATURAL DEATH

Our grief can be influenced by how difficult the death was and how the dying person reacted. Your relationship to the deceased will affect your grief. Many people feel guilty and reproach themselves for a long time if they think they didn't settle differences or they were not present when the person died.

GRIEVING OVER A SUDDEN DEATH

A sudden death, either from natural causes or an accident, is usually harder to accept than one following a long illness. Although a long illness can be depleting for relatives and friends, they have time to adjust to the inevitability of death. They also might be exhausted physically and emotionally enough to let go when death does come. However, if someone we care about is well one minute and then dead the next, we have no time for farewells.

This can mean we are left with unfinished business – things we'd like to have said and done to put closure on the valued relationship. We feel robbed of an opportunity. We can blame ourselves for not having always 'done the right thing', said 'I love you' often enough, or resolved an old issue we'd been meaning to address. We can feel guilty, angry, reproachful – and cheated. As one widow confided to me following her husband's accidental death at work: *'I said good-bye to him that morning, you know, the way you do, very casually. I expected to see him that night. I didn't know that good-bye was going to be forever'.*

GRIEVING OVER A VIOLENT DEATH

A violent death – death by murder – leaves the grieving person with many unresolved issues. Again, as with an unexpected death, there was no time to say good-bye. There may be guilt and self-reproach experienced for being a survivor, when a loved one has been killed. Much depends on the context in which the violent death took place. However, the aftermath of dealing with police, attending inquests and trials can add to the burden of working through the grief. Sometimes, years later, intense feelings and old pain can be stirred up with yet another legal hearing. The grieving person's stress and trauma may be increased by the intrusion of unwanted media interest. The grieving person may feel very out-of-control. Anniversaries of the crime bring back the pain and anger, hurt and sadness. Some people have reported that their grief-work felt as if it was impeded because the killer was not apprehended. They felt there was unfinished business – and they found it difficult to put closure on their experience.

GRIEVING OVER SUICIDE

It has been said that of all forms of death, suicide is the hardest for those left behind to come to terms with and do their good grief-work. In some ways, grieving a suicide is unique and different from grieving other deaths. For some people, the normal grief responses appear to be magnified. Usually, the unexpected suddenness of the event increases the shock and stress of grief. The severity of the shock can set off a frightening riot of emotions – long repressed memories, taboo thoughts and bizarre wishes. When the person left behind realises that suicide means their relative or friend was so unhappy that they actually sought death, their sadness – and often, ambivalence – are deepened. The tearing feelings of acute grief can be heightened by the terrible mixture of guilt, shame and blame. A survivor may become obsessed with the thought that the suicide might have been prevented – and they might punish themselves for this fantasied failing.

The grieving person may experience intense anger towards the person who committed suicide, sometimes seeing it as an act of punishment. The most extreme manifestation of this phenomenon was illustrated in the case where the estranged husband killed himself while on the phone to his wife. After the chronic abuse she experienced in their relationship, she made her escape. However, he was unable to let go and continued to intrude into her life. She interpreted this final act as one of ultimate abuse.

The grieving person may feel very guilty, particularly if they parted with the deceased on bad terms. If there was a quarrel the guilt is likely to be great. One woman felt intensely guilty for years after she ordered her son from the house and he drove his motor bike into a brick wall. There had been a history of abuse and violence by her son towards her. Over the years, she had made attempts to understand his behaviour and make allowances for it – after all, he was mentally ill. However, on the day she told him to leave if his attitude didn't improve, she had had enough. For years, she continued to reconstruct the events of that day, searching for the warning signs that she believed she overlooked. Like others who are left with unfinished business, she felt a sense of failure and rejection.

The sense of guilt is inescapable: 'If only I'd done (or said) so and so…', 'If only I'd realised how he felt…', 'If only she'd told me, I would have…', and 'If only I hadn't been away at that conference…'. The reality is that, although such statements carry genuine sentiments, they are after the event.

The reality is that such statements, even if uttered at the time, may not have made any difference to the outcome. We often have difficulty understanding why someone would want to commit suicide. Why would someone voluntarily cut his or her life short? However, the person who makes that decision, had their reasons. Oftentimes, what is perceived to be a genuinely unbearable life, for whatever reason, will be the deciding factor. It's important to remember that that decision was made by the person who took his or her life – and not the grieving survivor. Nevertheless, the survivor's mind might still reel from the pain of opportunities squandered, of harsh or unkind words spoken and of the promises that were made in good faith, but not kept.

For many people, the perceived stigma after a suicide is very traumatic. Some people cover up the fact that it was a suicide. Identifying the body, often cleaning up the scene of the suicide, answering police questions about the death can add to the stress and trauma.

There are no easy answers regarding how a grieving person might begin to heal their broken heart. It is a comfort to know that it is not unusual to feel grief in certain instances that lasts for years. Two or three years of grieving are not unusual. Knowledge brings comfort and hope that the strange kaleidoscope that is grief will pass. It also is important to know that there are common initial responses that might help us validate and 'normalise' our own experience.

WHEN SOMEONE DIES

OUR INITIAL RESPONSES

When someone close to us dies, the thoughts and emotions that sweep over us form a wild and disordered kaleidoscope. The first few days after the death may only be remembered through a rolling mist which occasionally permits glimpses of a blurred landscape of actions and feelings. These first few days and even the first week, following the shock of the news of the death of someone for whom we care, resemble a tranquillised state. This initial stage of grief is experienced as a half-life with flashes of terrible pain. The death comes as a shock, whether it was the result of a long-standing illness or a sudden death.

Shock, numbness and confusion may be Nature's way of covering the grieving person with a protective emotional blanket. This emotional blanket is removed when the grieving person faces the terrible fact that their loved one is gone forever. Often people wonder that they 'have no feelings' when the death occurs. A numbness moves in to envelope them so fast that they are unaware of their first reaction.

Colin Murray Parkes, the British psychiatrist and researcher recalls one widow in his London study who told him of a short lived explosion before the numbness set in: *'I was aware of a horrible wailing and knew it was me.'*

Some people have described how they almost lost contact with themselves for a short moment – before numbness set in. One man described this sensation– in his case, an explosion of words: *'No! No! You can't leave me alone!'* – as if *'I was seeing myself from a distance'* and then numbness descended. This man experienced a dissociative sensation – he was watching the scene as well as being in the scene.

When the world becomes chaotic and unsafe, we may prefer to turn inward and focus on our roller-coaster thoughts and feelings. C. S. Lewis in *A Grief Observed*, said,

> *'There is a sort of invisible blanket between the world and me. I find it hard to take in what anyone says. Or perhaps hard to want to take it in. It is so uninteresting. Yet I want others to be about me. I dread the moments when the house is empty. If only they would talk to one another and not to me.'*

In this initial period there may be weeping and wailing and a high degree of agitation. Only later does the grieving person realise how disturbing this period was, how their memory failed and how they mislaid or lost things. Lily Pincus, a social worker and founder of the Marital Studies at London's famous Tavistock Institute, recalls how during these first confusing days following her husband's death, she picked up important papers from his attorney. Then she threw them into a strange letter box.

During these first few days, people often report either extreme lethargy – or overactivity.

There may also be regression during this period. This is normal, but can appear to be frightening to many people – particularly those concerned about the grieving person. Lily Pincus tells of one grieving woman who wrapped herself in a soaking hot bath towel, and curled up in her favourite chair in fetal position. This sort of regressive behaviour serves a purpose – it is comforting. For this woman, it meant she could go on and perform her part in her husband's memorial service.

OUR SUBSEQUENT RESPONSES

When the protective numbness is gone, a grieving person is left with the twin facts of a death and continuing life. Waves of mixed emotions may sweep over a person – longing, anxiety, guilt, anger – the psyche is trying to incorporate the reality of the death and to accept the new situation of life without that person.

Often there is irritability and restlessness, inability to concentrate, to sleep, with too much eating or too little. People may have very vivid, often disturbing dreams, of the person whom they have lost. People report loneliness and sadness and loss of interest in the world. Sometimes there are attacks of panic and waves of crying.

One woman, Catherine, 48, whose husband died in a car accident, despaired that she would never stop grieving and heal. She says,

'How long is this awful pain going to last? I thought I was doing well. But here I am – five months later and I'm a wreck. I can't seem to stop crying.'

Occasionally there is an attempt to rewrite history – to change past relationships and what happened. This is a form of wishful thinking.

Moving from an acute phase of grief, people say that their episodes of sadness are less frequent and last for shorter periods. Memories of the deceased are recalled with nostalgia and warmth instead of just sadness and pain. But this process of moving from acute grief towards good grief is a slow one – moving in fits and starts.

The turning point may be reached just when you think you can't stand another day in limbo. You might wake up and feel a little more hopeful. This first glimmer of hope is a sign that you are ready to decide to move forward with your life.

However, just as a person is seemingly moving towards recovery, there might be a relapse – either spontaneously, or with reason. A relapse often is associated with an anniversary or special holiday or event.

Relapses happen and it is only by recognising their raw distress and full force – and the knowledge that they will pass – do they appear l ess frightening.

Obsessive ruminations are a necessary part of working through your grief. These ruminations can be frightening. These may be part of our initial response and continue in a sporadic way for weeks or even months. People often say, 'Thoughts of her never leave me', or 'He is constantly on my mind.'

However, with good grief-work, the relapses occur less and less often. When someone asks: 'How long will it go on?' the answer is not obvious. People are different. Some people may take a year, for others it may take two or three. One woman said that it was her belief that when a mother loses a child, the grief is virtually permanent.

BAD TIMES FOR GRIEF

Any grieving person will tell you that there are certain 'bad times' for them. These are times of the day, week, month or year when the person finds they suffer more distress. At first, these bad times surprise the grieving person. They are unprepared. However, if you understand the association between these bad times and your memories, you can work to easing your pain.

People often say that waking in the morning and bedtimes are the worst times. Special occasions also can be bad times – memories and grief feelings come flooding back at holiday times, major celebrations, at the first sign of spring or the first snow – and on anniversary dates. These anniversary dates are the anniversary of the person's departure or death and their birthday. Other days can be just as sad, for example, celebrating family get-togethers and Mother's or Father's Day in their absence.

Eventually, these bad times will recede and be replaced with only passing pain and a sense of affection and nostalgia in the memories.

A DEATH IN THE FAMILY

The majority of us spend our early, formative years in a family group of some sort. For better or worse, this group provides us with the human essentials – our basic physical needs and an opportunity to learn from others. Whatever the size or composition of this family group – the loss of one member will have consequences for everyone within it. While each person will struggle to cope with their own personal loss, at the same time, they also will have to deal with the loss suffered by other members of the family.

The parent-child bond is one of the longest ties of our lives. Our parents are part of us and we are part of them.

THE DEATH OF A MOTHER

Changing attitudes have meant that parenting a young child is a responsibility for both mother and father. Families today mostly strive for equal responsibility. Recent surveys however, have indicated that it is still the mother who will do the majority of the feeding, bathing and nurturing which all children need to grow into healthy human beings.

Mothers have many roles and responsibilities: homemaker, nurturer, educationalist, family peace-maker, nurse and comforter and friend. A mother's influence is considerable.

To lose a mother is to lose the person who cared for us in a special way. To lose a mother means no-one else will ever *mother* us in quite the same way again. Along with the grief of your mother's death, you will grieve the loss of mothering itself. It may be many years since your mother last cuddled you or kissed your hurts better, but, like a small child, something inside you will cry out for the loss of that love. For a while, you'll experience the world as a colder and harder place because of the absence of that love.

When we lose our mother we lose the person who gave us life – literally.

When a daughter loses a mother

When a daughter loses a mother, the gender chain that links the generations is broken.

A special kind of loss is experienced. Whether your mother was 'good' or only 'good enough', a daughter will miss the woman who has been an essential part of her life.

Some mothers and daughters are very close. Some women truly believe that they are 'best friends' with their mothers. Because best friends share problems and are there when you need them, a daughter who is also a friend, will doubly miss her mother. Her mother indeed, has been a special person. When her mother dies, the daughter finds she doesn't have the same special understanding with anyone else, nor can she go shopping with such a supportive woman, nor discuss the merits and demerits of boyfriends, commiserate with her or share her joys.

If the daughter has had a difficult relationship with her mother, death destroys any chance of reconciliation. It is not uncommon for mothers and daughters to clash in the stressful teenage years and sometimes to go on clashing. Sometimes a mother may die before such conflict can be understood and reconciled. Inevitably in such a case, there will be regrets.

A son loses a mother

When a son loses his mother, he loses part of his history. He loses a unique relationship with a woman who played a major role in the creation of the person he is and has become. It is through his mother that a son first learns about the world.

Until a son reaches the age when he connects with young women, his mother may be the only link with women and through her he will learn about the world of emotions and senses. She might be the only one who understands that 'big boys' need to cry sometimes.

A mother's nurturing, giving, motherly love is unique – as is her unconditional love – no-one will ever love him in quite that way again. Depending on his age at the time of her death, a son may have difficulties in expressing his grief. If he is already a young man, he might see himself in the stereotyped solver-of-problems male role. There is no solution to grief. Grief is the experience he will have to live through.

THE DEATH OF A FATHER

The death of a father is unique in its own way. The relationship between this man and you can never be repeated. You have seen a side of him which will not be apparent to his colleagues or even his friends. One way or another, a father has been a part of your existence since birth. Genetically and behaviourally, he has influenced you and that influence will continue after his death.

Fathers have to live up to many expectations in our society. They may be the principal bread-winner contributing towards the financial security and well-being of the family. Fathers may have the role of 'rule-maker' and although this is changing, it might be the case in many families. From fathers we may learn how the world of rules and the world, in general, works. Fathers may be able to help you get things back in perspective when your thinking about life is lob-sided and out of proportion.

In everyday life, fathers have their uses and you remember as a child that he was the chief car driver, who picked you up and dropped you off at parties, school and tap dance classes.

A daughter loses a father

The relationship between a father and daughter changes over the years. To some fathers, their daughter is the little princess. To lose such a special relationship is to lose so much. There are other relationships where the father is strict and controlling and the daughter grows apart, and with time, fights hard for her right to freedom. Most father-daughter relationships are between these two extremes. Many daughters believe that when they lose their father, they lose the one man who had the potential to – and often did – love them unconditionally.

A son loses a father

The relationship between a father and son changes – often dramatically over the years. Much of these changes are dictated by the personalities of the two men – their similarities and differences. For many young men, their fathers are their role-models and friends. There might be a very close bond. There is no substitute for such a loss. The world may seem a less secure place without the love, knowledge and companionship of a father.

ON BECOMING AN ORPHAN

Although the popular image of an orphan is that of a small waif lost in a large, hostile institution, we can be orphaned in many different ways. We don't have to be small or young to be orphaned. There are lots of orphaned adults – people who have lost both their parents.

The age at which we lose one or both parents plays a part in our grieving. The longer we have our parents with us, the more comfortable we feel, and sometimes believe we'll have them with us forever. It can come as a huge shock when we are suddenly in the world without them. However, the younger we are when we are orphaned the more vulnerable we really are. Children have a stronger attachment to their parents, in so much as they still rely on them practically and emotionally, almost exclusively. The loss of a parent or parents when we are young leaves us feeling our security has gone. Our support is no longer there and we must fend for ourselves.

Becoming an orphan means the end of childhood, even though the orphan may still technically be a child. It brings to an end one part of their lives. Becoming an orphan means possibly losing our history. Our parents retain the memories of our infancy and childhood in their minds. When they die they take these memories with them. We may feel the loss greatly when no-one now knows what time of day we were born, or whether we had measles or mumps. If we are lucky, we might have other family members to fill in the gaps. But there is no substitute for parents in answering the hundred and one little questions we wish to have answered.

Emily Dickinson wrote in **The Belle of Amburst**, *'Hold your parents tenderly, for the world will seem a strange and distant place when they are gone.'*

Our parents are our buffers and as we approach midlife, we become aware that our parents are growing older. Many of us experience an element of anticipatory grief for our parents' inevitable death, and with it, perhaps anxiety and fear about our own ageing and death.

Anne Sexton, the famous poet, known for her 'confessional' style of poetry became an orphan, at the age of 31, in a space of three months in 1959. Her poem, **_The Truth the Dead Know_** tells us of her experience:

The Truth the Dead Know

For my mother, born March 1902, died March 1959,
and my father, born February, 1900, died June 1959

Gone, I say and walk from church,
refusing the stiff procession to the grave,
letting the dead ride alone in the hearse.
It is June. I am tired of being brave.

We drive to the Cape. I cultivate
myself where the sun gutters from the sky,
where the sea swings in like an iron gate
and we touch. In another country people die.

My darling, the wind falls in like stones
from the whitehearted water and when we touch
we enter touch entirely. No one's alone,
Men kill for this, or for as much.

And what of the dead? They lie without shoes
in their stone boats. They are more like stone
than the sea would be if it stopped. They refuse
to be blessed, throat, eye and knucklebone.

THE DEATH OF GRANDPARENTS

Often, in childhood, the death of a grandparent is the first death we will experience. Grandparents are special people, and many young people have close relationships with one or both grandparents – on one or both sides of the family. Many children look forward to visits with pleasure, because the grandparents make such a fuss of them. They feel special with grandma and grandpa. Telephone calls are eagerly awaited and letters and cards sent to keep in touch. Even where the grandparents are more distant figures, they will assume importance in a child's life at certain holiday times and celebrations.

During the adolescent years, many teenagers find a natural allay in a grandparent. In disputes with parents, having a grandparent on your side can be a powerful strategy. Losing a grandparent is a personal loss and a loss for your parents. Such a death marks an end of an era and the good memories will become part of the family history.

> **PROMPT FOR YOUR PEN**

Exercise   **Exploring your relationships and your losses**

Reflect on your relationships with your family members.

How would you describe these relationships? With parents? With grandparents? With brothers and sisters? With uncles and aunts? With cousins?

Have you lost an important person?

How would you describe the losses you experienced?

DEATH OF A CHILD

Children are our future, and they are supposed to outlive their parents. The natural pattern of life is that the old give way to the young. People often comment that it is sad, but somehow natural to lose through death an elderly person, but it is intensely sad and unnatural to lose a child.

It has been said that no death is so sad as the death of a child. It has been said that no parent ever gets over the grief of losing a child – the grief is a life-long process. Some parents have spoken about the 'loss without end' and how they keep a hidden calendar in their minds. They make a mental note of the date when the child would have been 16, 21, 30 and all the birthdays and special days are remembered. The death of a baby, a stillbirth, a cot death is a cruel loss. It is hard to accept the reality of such a loss – a baby born to die. The question, 'Why did it die?' is a question that continues to haunt.

The death of a child, whether an infant, or the child of 45 whose parent is now 68, is an 'all wrong' death. It goes against the rules.

Read the following case study. It is about a mother, Suse Lowenstein, whose son was killed on Pan Am flight 103, which crashed over Lockerbie, Scotland, killing all 270 people on board.

Flight 103

When Alex Lowenstein, 21, was home from University for the summer vacation of 1988, he willingly posed for his mother, a New York sculptor. Three figures of the virile young surfer were sufficiently completed for his mother to continue her work, using photographs, while Alexander spent the autumn studying in London.

He was due home for Christmas, but at the beginning of December he had a surprise visit from his mother. Suse had felt that she just must see her son and she had dropped everything to travel to London for what turned out to be a wonderful week of sightseeing with him.

On December 21, Suse was working on her sculpture, knowing that Alex's plane would have left London and that he would soon be home! Then the phone rang. A friend of Alex's wanted to know his Pan Am flight number.

'103,' Suse replied.

'Oh my God, haven't you heard? That plane just exploded over Scotland,' cried the friend. Stunned, Suse reprimanded the girl for playing a morbid joke. Then she collapsed. 'I knew,' she says, 'that Alexander was dead.'

The next time Suse saw Alexander was in a dream, three days after the crash. 'I was working in my studio, and he was leaning against the door frame,' she says. 'His face was very white, and he was begging me not to let him go. I woke up and was beside myself.'

Suse's despair turned to rage about a news report that the American Embassy in Finland had been tipped off by an anonymous phone caller in early December that terrorists were planning to bomb a Pan Am plane in Europe. U.S. diplomatic personnel were informed of the threat so that they could adjust their Christmas travel plans. Pan Am was also notified, but chose not to tell its customers.

It was the cold end of January before Alexander's remains were returned to America. At Kennedy International Airport the Lowensteins and other grieving families gathered at an area used for handling livestock.

'The rear of the truck opened, and they started unloading coffins with a fork lift,' Suse recalls. 'That's all. Neither Pan Am nor the U.S. Government sent a representative. They showed us no dignity or respect.'

By contrast, Suse is grateful to the Scottish police and people of Lockerbie for their heartfelt condolences and their efforts to recover the personal effects of the victims.

'It may seem bizarre,' she says, 'but I've found myself hungering for every little piece of him.' The grisly mementos include torn clothing, half a camera and torn ID cards.' The two halves of Alexander's suitcase landed more than 64 kilometres apart, and his windcheater was found 96 kilometres from Lockerbie. Every item was returned washed and hand wrapped.

In the months following the bombing, Suse discovered that working on her sculptures of Alexander helped her to make him whole again in her mind.

The finished work is a ring of eight sorrowing figures encircling a woman with one arm draped protectively over her womb and the other stretched heavenward in a gesture of despair.

Suse's greatest fear is that she will somehow forget her son. 'I need to speak about him,' she says. Her husband Peter has grieved quite differently. He finds it painful to talk about Alexander and values the quiet times alone, flying in his single-engine Piper Dakota.

Both Suse and Peter have been active in a committee formed by relatives of Pan Am Flight 103 victims to lobby for improved airport security measures

*and to monitor the continuing criminal investigation of the bombing.
In August 1991, Peter was part of a delegation that met with British
transportation officials and the Scottish police.*

Adapted from Glassock and Rowling, 1992

PROMPT FOR YOUR PEN

Exercise   **Reflecting on the case of Flight 103**

Re-read the case study and consider the following questions:
In what ways do you see Alex's mother, Suse working on her tasks of grieving?
What might account for the differences in grieving between Suse and Peter?

It is interesting to note that grieving people sometimes report dreaming
about the deceased. Dreams are a way of processing our feelings of grief and
in dreams, people often say they see themselves saying good-bye to their
loved one and this can be accompanied by feelings of letting go.

In Suse's case, she dreamt of Alex soon after the crash. In her dream, he
was begging her not to let him go. Because Suse's grief is new at that stage,
she is unable to accept that Alex is really dead. Her dream represents a
beginning – on working on the first task of accepting the reality of the loss.

HEALING COMES FROM REMEMBERING

It is clear that Suse will always remember her son. So will her husband.
Yet their ways of dealing with his death – and remembering him – will be
different.

In Judith Guest's novel, ***Ordinary People***, the remaining family
members have different ways of remembering – and for them, the crisis ends
in their going their separate ways.

When seventeen-year-old Conrad Jarrett's life is spared in a boating
accident that takes his older brother's life, the story that unfolds reveals
the complexity of human relationships in families and the impact of the

death of a son – and brother. The impact of this death means something different for each family member. Judith Guest's writing reveals that with the marriage and family ties already strained, the death of one son acts to deepen these difficulties.

To the outside world, Conrad's parents, Calvin and Beth Jarrett, are seen as successful and competent people. The Jarretts seem to have it all worked out. Yet, Beth and Calvin are deeply troubled people. Beth, as the mother, has played favourites and had chosen Buck, the son killed on the lake, to bless. After the accident, she finds herself unable to cope with the reality of her life in ruins. Her favourite son is dead. Her husband, Calvin feels helpless as he watches the two people closest to him hurting, but out of his reach.

They all have their separate memories – they all remember Buck differently.

Conrad, as the surviving son, feels different from other students at his high school and he tells his psychiatrist, Dr. Berger, that he wants to be rid of his guilt feelings. As an accident survivor, he is haunted by guilty dreams and memories. He dearly wants to get rid of the past and become an ordinary teenager again.

The novel ends with the Jarretts breaking up – at least temporarily. Beth leaves Calvin and returns to her brother's home in Houston. Conrad asks his father, *'How did everything fall apart like this?'* Calvin answers his son, *'It's nobody's fault...It is the way things are.'* Being ordinary, average does not mean that we don't have self-doubts, and that loss and grief will not touch us.

However, one lesson from this story for us all concerns the need to allow ourselves to be weaned from one set of attachments and force ourselves to let go and find a new path for the future.

John Bramblett in his book, ***When Good-bye is Forever: Learning to Live Again After the Loss of a Child***, writes about the necessity to remember – yet, let go – if a parent is do their good grief-work. He and his wife lost their youngest child, a boy aged two in an accident. He writes,

'While letting go is not easy or pleasant, it is essential to working our way through grief and ultimately resolving it. Where letting go does not occur, the grieving consumes the mourner's energy, leaving life in a state of suspended animation.

Make no mistake about it: letting go is frightening. We may well face an overwhelming assault of guilt that screams at us, 'you are abandoning your child!' The emotional attack is substantial. Should we let laughter return to our lives or should we continue to grieve? If we start to let go, won't we also start to forget the little details of the child who lives in our memory – details that are really all that we have left now? Won't they slip away, just as the child has done, as we begin to accept the loss? And so we struggle with the problem – our human nature wanting to hold onto every tangible and intangible trace our child has left behind – while inside us a still, small voice tells us that we must let go or we, too, will be lost.'

Perhaps with this most difficult of deaths – the loss of a child – healing comes not from forgetting, but from remembering – and ultimately – letting go, whilst still remembering as John Bramblett suggests.

You will recall, that in earlier times parents, and in particular mothers, were encouraged to 'forget' their stillborn babies. The same advice was dispensed in the case of the loss of an infant through cot death. Today, there is greater awareness and open encouragement for parents to become actively involved in fare-welling their dead babies.

When a couple loses a baby, the great mysteries of birth and death come at almost the same time. A growing number of institutions have grief counselling and support groups for parents who have lost a baby to miscarriage, stillbirth or other perinatal complications. It is important for parents to do their good grief-work around such a loss – not to forget, but to remember – and ultimately to let go.

LOSS OF A SPOUSE OR PARTNER

Along with the loss of a child, it is said that the loss of a partner or spouse is the greatest loss we can experience. It is the loss that breaks many connections: the partnership is dissolved and half of us is gone. When Herb lost his wife, after a long illness, he was so distraught that his children urged him to seek professional help. Herb says,

'When my wife died, I don't remember too much about it. My children tell me I went into a state of shock. Maybe I was in this state for a week – I don't know. I knew she was dying, but when it happened – well, I just went blank. People came to see me at home, but I can't remember who they were. About a week later, it hit me – this is the way it was going to be – this is the way it was – I didn't have my wife anymore. It felt like someone had cut off my left arm.'

Some people describe how they feel heart-broken and how empty their lives feel when a partner dies. If the relationship has been a long and successful one, the pain may be great. For many people, the emotional dependence leaves them feeling empty, abandoned and frustrated in often futile efforts to find ways to fill the void.

WHEN BONDS ARE BROKEN

Again, C. S. Lewis in his well-known account of personal agony after losing his wife, illuminates the essence of grief felt by the surviving partner,

'They tell me H. is happy now, they tell me she is at peace. What makes them so sure of this? I don't mean that I fear the worst of all…But why are they so sure that all anguish ends with death?…Why should the separation that so agonizes the lover who is left behind be painless to the lover who departs?… We are under the harrow and can't escape. Reality, looked at steadily, is unbearable…How often – will it be for always? – how often will the vast emptiness astonish me like a complete novelty and make me say, 'I never realized my loss till this moment'? The same leg is cut off time after time. The first plunge of the knife into the flesh is felt again and again…Grief is like a long valley, a winding valley where any bend may reveal a totally new landscape.'

People who have lost their partners often speak in the imagery of Herb and C. S. Lewis. They speak about being broken-hearted, of losing parts of themselves, the loss being akin to losing a limb.

Losing a partner means losing all the emotional support, friendship and companionship you had, and still having to find ways to fulfil your tasks and responsibilities. This is difficult in situations where there are young children still at home, and the surviving partner and parent has to fulfill roles and perform alone and often unsupported, unfamiliar roles and responsibilities.

Grief, for the surviving partner can feel like a conglomerate of deprivations and responsibilities, as well as painful in its actual physical and emotional separation. This separation means eating alone, sleeping alone and caring for the children alone. Loneliness and deprivation may become the key experiences in people's lives.

THE DECISION TO LIVE

People report that one of the most difficult decisions they face is determining whether they had the will to begin again. One 64-year-old widow described how afraid she was to 'start over'. Yet, from somewhere within herself, she found a little strength to call a few friends and suggest meeting for lunch. This was one month after her husband died. She had not been ready to see people, to make any contact with people before this time. For this woman, the very act of getting out seemed to add some new energy and she spoke cautiously about how she might be able to open herself up to some new possibilities – eventually. Her decision to live, was tempered by her sense of guilt for choosing to make a start.

Letting go of your partner is difficult, but it needs to be done, in order to make that decision to start living – to start over.

One important step is to re-enter the world and re-connect with friends or to make new connections. Attending a support group and hearing the stories of other people in a similar situation can prove very empowering. Seeing the progress of others in the group can provide us with hope that we might actually get through this sad experience and emerge on the other side of grief.

After losing a partner, many people vow that they will never enter another permanent relationship. However, as they move towards healing their hearts, they become more aware of their need to assuage their loneliness. Entering a replacement relationship becomes a viable alternative for many people. Research indicates that many people do enter a new relationship about two years after their loss.

Practice wisdom from counsellors and therapists also indicates that such replacement relationships will be more sound if they are entered after the person has given themselves time to heal before thinking of beginning the new relationship.

Losing a partner changes us. There is no way we will ever be the same person again. In a sense, we will have a new identity. Our values have changed. Grief has changed us.

People need time to slip out of one shell before growing another. When you are ready, you will know that grief is behind you and a new life is ahead.

A DEATH OUTSIDE THE FAMILY

Not all the people we love and care about are in our family. There will be people in all our lives who have shared common interests with us and part of our lives has been enriched by our relationship with them.

It may not be until we lose such a person that we become fully aware of the importance they had in our life. When they die we might find ourselves viewing ourselves and the world a little differently. Each loss will have its own special significance for us. As young people, the death of a teacher can affect us profoundly. A teacher is an important person in our lives, they might be the first person to see our potential and encourage us to reach for the stars. When a boss dies, our position in the organisation may be threatened – and we may miss that person's management style. The loss of a lover from our past may turn our thoughts back to that time and we might find ourselves grieving its loss as well as the person who has died.

There are times in life when we meet people with whom we appear to have a natural affinity. If a person we care about and would like to know better dies, we feel cheated. They could have become a very important part of our lives and we might feel we have been robbed of an opportunity to develop a meaningful relationship.

THE DEATH OF A FRIEND

Most of us have at least one good friend. Most of us recognise that having a good friend is important to our lives. We all know what a friend is: someone with whom we can share our thoughts and feelings, someone who cares for us and for whom we would walk on hot coals. Friendship is a relationship based on equality, although even in good friendships there will be temporary imbalances, ups and downs, separations and changes of fortune – but a good friendship will survive all these.

We choose to spend time with our friends, so that the relationship is built on choice. As the old adage says, 'We may not choose our family but we do choose our friends.'

It is this very special relationship that vanishes when a friend dies. We may be shocked, confused, sad, angry, distressed – and all these grief feelings will need to be worked through.

When we lose a best friend, the sort of friend who knows things about us that other people wouldn't suspect, the loss is devastating. If we have known them for a long time, they carry part of our history with them, they have been part of our changes and we always thought they would be there in our lives in the future.

To lose such a precious friend is to lose a part of ourselves.

———————

PART III

THE CHALLENGE OF CHANGE:

GRIEF INTO GROWTH, LOSS INTO GAIN

One knows what one has lost,
but not what one may find.

GEORGE SAND [The Haunted Pool, 1851]

7

FROM BAD GRIEF TO GOOD GRIEF

The only way through pain... is to absorb, probe,
understand exactly what it is and what it means.
To close the door on pain is to miss the chance for
growth... Nothing that happens to us, even the most
terrible shock, is unusable, and everything has somehow
to be built into the fabric of the personality.

MAY SARTON [Recovering: A Journal 1978-1979]

Grieving is a major stressor. We all know how stress can suppress the immune system and make us more vulnerable to infection and disease. How does this happen? Stress is associated with the release of chemicals into the bloodstream from the glands of the endocrine system. Some reactions that occur with stress include the release of:

- cortisol, which leads to reduced immunity or resistance to illness
- adrenaline, which leads to increased blood pressure and heightened energy levels
- an increase in fatty substances into the blood, which may lead to narrowing of the arteries, and an increase in cholesterol

J. William Worden found in his work with grieving people that they report experiences and reactions that are physical in nature. These include:

- oversensitivity to noise
- tightness in the chest or hollowness in the stomach
- breathlessness
- lack of energy
- dry mouth
- muscular weakness
- loss of appetite
- sleep disturbance
- headaches
- disturbance in the menstrual cycle
- disturbances of digestion
- increase in a range of illnesses e.g. asthma, ulcers and skin complaints

As mentioned in an earlier chapter, some studies have suggested that some cancers, heart attacks and even adult onset diabetes may be triggered by unresolved grief. It is important to emphasise here that unresolved grief did not cause these illnesses, because there has to be an underlying predisposition. However, there appear to be strong associations between unresolved grief and illness.

Common physical complaints grieving people report include digestive problems, disturbed sleep, loss of appetite, exhaustion. Grieving can be hard work, so the rhythms of the body are disturbed. However, such physical reactions should be restored to normal with good grief-work.

GRIEF AS STRESS

If we understand that grief is stressful, we can better comprehend and accept the uncomfortable bodily sensations and responses we are experiencing. It is reassuring that such sensations and responses are normal and that we are not going mad, as we sometimes suspect we are. The challenge of good grief-work is to find ways of expressing and managing our feelings and reactions.

In some cultures, activity is encouraged to dissipate the energy and stress a grieving person feels. For instance, lengthy wailing periods use up a lot of energy in grieving. This might well help to use the excess adrenaline in the body. Encouraging inactivity and sleep may not be so stress reducing. It is important to re-emphasise the research on the benefits of 'having a good cry'. Remember that the chemical composition of tears caused by emotional crying is different from other tears. Some researchers believe that these tears remove toxic substances and help return the body to equilibrium.

For some people, who are uncomfortable with emotional issues, it is reassuring to know that there are valid physical reasons supporting the release of grief. This helps validate them in their grief.

PROMPT FOR YOUR PEN

Exercise **Reflecting on stressful times**

Think back to a time when you felt very stressed. The stress need not be related to loss. The stress could be related to any life event, for example, stressful times at work meeting deadlines.

• How did you know you were stressed?
• What were some of the indicators that you were stressed?

In the example about stressful times at work, a person's physical responses might be to tense their upper back, hunch their shoulders and possibly develop neck pain or headaches. They might have negative thoughts such as 'I'm not good enough – I'll never meet the deadline'. They might feel frustrated, angry and powerless. In terms of behaviour, the person might be irritable at work and easily upset at home. This example shows us how a stressful event clearly has effects and consequences in our lives.

MEASURING STRESS

Before looking at how we might measure stress it's important to point out that the following scale and interpretation is a guideline only. As we know, people respond to stress differently. Each person has their own unique threshold for stress and coping mechanisms. However, the following scale, devised by Holmes and Rahe is a good starting point for measuring the 'strength' of certain life changes. The *Holmes-Rahe Survey of Recent Experiences* is also called the Social Readjustment Rating Scale. It gives an indication as to the stress associated with traumatic life events. It aims to 'measure' the degree of disruption to the life-style and regular routine of the person concerned.

In the Holmes-Rahe scale, stressful events are assigned a numerical value, that reflects their relative impact. It is theorised that stress induced by these events can not only seriously affect a person's health, but that it is also cumulative. For example, a person who has recently divorced and changed their living conditions will score 73 plus 25 Life Change Units (LCUs) which is seen as suffering about an equivalent amount of stress as someone who has lost a partner, which at 100 LCUs is seen as the greatest stressor. Someone suffering several stressful events in quick succession would be considered to be at higher risk of a stress-related illness. Such a person, if dealing with more than one consecutive or parallel loss, might have greater difficulty in doing their grief-work. They are candidates for complicated grief – or being 'stuck' in their good grief-work.

Holmes-Rahe Survey of Recent Experiences
(Social Readjustment Rating Scale: SRRS)

Life events	Life change units (LCUs)
Death of a spouse*	100
Divorce	73
Marital separation	65
Death of close family member	63
Personal injury or illness	53
Marriage	50
Fired at work	47
Retirement	45
Change in health of family member	44

Pregnancy	40
Sexual difficulties	39
Change in financial state	38
Death of close friend	37
Change to different line of work	36
Change in living conditions	25
Trouble with boss	23
Change in residence	20

* You might realise that death of a child is not included in this survey. However, some researchers and grief counsellors believe it to be rated close to, if not a little higher than, death of a spouse.

This scale gives us some idea about the impact of certain changes and losses. Contained within these changes and losses are associated losses, for example, loss of identity, loss of self-esteem, feelings of powerlessness, and depression.

A lack of recognition of loss is also a source of stress. This lack of recognition heralds grief that has gone wrong.

A NOTE ABOUT LIFELONG GRIEF

It has been said that although prolonged grief is abnormal, lifelong grief may be normal, in some cases.

Experts believe that the loss of a child, especially a young child or adolescent, is not only a grief that has the longest lasting effects, but also that it is perfectly normal for the parents, and particularly the mother, to grieve permanently. As one mother asked me: *'How can you ever get over your child dying?'*

However, this kind of lifelong grief does not necessarily interfere with life, even though the pain, the memories and the yearning may continue. A father, whose 16-year-old son left home and had not been seen nor heard from for 10 years said, *'My ache and pain is as deep and sharp as ever. I still see my son as clearly as ever.'*

Researchers have found that many widows too, may grieve permanently for their husbands. Expressions such as *'I'll never forget him'* and *'He's still with me'* are often heard.

WHEN GRIEF GOES WRONG

Some people are afraid of facing loss because they are afraid of getting into a state that reminds them of a time when as children, they were helpless and dependent on other people. It is frightening for an adult to regress and feel once more like a small and helpless child. Other people are able to embark on their good grief-work, or alternatively, move through their journey to recovery. For some, however, their grief-work gets 'stuck'. They are unable to move through the tasks of grieving.

Remember: the tasks of grief-work involve:

(i) accepting that the loss is a reality
(ii) entering into the emotions of grief
(iii) acquiring new skills
(iv) reinvesting energy in new people and new ways

Unresolved grief manifests itself in several ways. It my be delayed or postponed, avoided, chronic or masked in nature.

DELAYED OR POSTPONED GRIEF

In delayed grief, at the time of the loss, a person may show signs of grief, but they are not commensurate with the seriousness of the loss. They appear to 'hold onto' themselves and ironically, may be congratulated for being so stoic. However, a person who delays grief attempts to keep the pain at a distance, most probably unconsciously. They have done their first task: acceptance of the loss as a reality, purely intellectually. There is an incomplete expression of sadness and an inability to enter into the second task: entering into the emotions of grief. This person may have cried a little at the funeral but in suppressing the liberating tears, might well have suppressed the healing forces as well.

Often in delayed grief, the person contrives busyness and this intense activity and restlessness distances the expression of pain and sadness. Some delayed grievers find themselves turning to physicians for frequent complaints. It is thought that this represents a displacement of the pain of the loss. One 64-year-old widow, said that she had experienced a severe skin conditions and when that cleared up, she began to complain of intestinal pain and when that was attended to the pain shifted to her back. Finally, the shifting pain from organ to organ was assessed to be related to her delayed grief response and she was sent for counselling.

Months or even years later, the person who delays grieving may find that a sad film, a holiday, a relatively minor loss, or even witnessing the loss and grief of others, will re-open their suppressed grief-work. Often this grief is felt intensely. One theory suggests that people respond with delayed grief, if they were unable to grieve fully at the time. They might have been unable to do so for whatever reason, perhaps because of other demands and responsibilities on him or her, or a confluence of several sources of stress as seen in the Life Change Units of the Holmes-Rahe scale. For instance, several coincidental or consecutive stresses might be a trigger for grief suppression.

AVOIDED GRIEF

In 1937, the psychoanalyst Helene Deutsch described avoided grief. This type of grief is variously called: repressed, unreleased, pathological and disguised. She suggested that if a grieving person does not fully express their feelings of grief, this will result in psychosomatic and psychological symptoms. She believed vague pains for which no organic cause can be found, as well as actual ailments like asthma, ulcers, headaches and so on, can develop. In addition, the grieving person might develop symptoms that resemble the illness of the deceased. Psychologically, she suggested that the person who avoids grief will be either strongly dependent on others or the reverse – totally isolated.

Some people may develop phobic behaviour towards anything that might remind them the deceased. For instance, all memories of the deceased may be removed, with the home being stripped of photographs and other reminders. Visits to the cemetery are avoided and sometimes there are suicide attempts and suicide.

Years after the loss, if such a person is exposed to another loss, for example, abandonment by a lover, a much more dramatic picture may emerge. The response to the abandonment seems to be out of all proportion, with all the person's thoughts centred on the lover and getting him or her back. The person can rarely understand their intense reaction and can be frightened by their response. On closer analysis, avoided grief becomes clear. Often the avoided grief is for a dead parent or other significant person. Sometimes this loss spans 40 years – as does the avoided grief – until another loss triggers it.

CHRONIC GRIEF

Chronic grief is the sort of grief that fills the grieving person's life and replaces almost everything else. Chronic grief continues for an excessive period of time, usually many years. Sometimes, the person realises they are 'stuck' in grief. It is believed that this type of grief response occurs when the person, at an unconscious level, cannot accept the reality of the loss.

An example of chronic grief is the case of Queen Victoria, who continued to conduct much of her life as if her husband, Prince Albert, were still alive. She was 'stuck' in her grief to the point that she was unable to be civil to her son, the Prince of Wales. Her violent anger towards her son was related to her belief that his escapades had led to Prince Albert's death. She blamed his death on the fact that he had to travel to Cambridge to deal with their son's improper behaviour. Prince Albert returned ill from the trip and died. Queen Victoria never forgave the Prince of Wales saying of him, *'It quite irritates me to see him in the room.'*

The chronic griever, unlike the person who avoids grief, will worship almost everything that has to do with the lost person or thing. It is not uncommon for the deceased's bedroom to remain untouched for years, their clothes may still hang in the wardrobe, and there may be pictures of the deceased everywhere. With chronic grief, a person may visit the cemetery frequently, almost obsessively.

On rare occasions, the chronic griever develops phobic behaviour, like that seen in avoided grief. The person may avoid the bedroom or keep away from memory-filled places so as not to trigger off pain and sadness.

After years of talking about nothing but the deceased, the chronic griever might find himself or herself bereft of friends. Many chronic grievers isolate themselves and become seemingly unapproachable in their pain-filled everyday lives.

Chronic grief is identified when the person is unable or unwilling to acquire new skills. Consequently, the person comes to a stand-still on the third task of grieving, but also has problems with the second task of grieving. While the grieving person may enter into the emotions of grief, they do so in such a rigid manner that they are not released. The chronic griever cannot move to the fourth task of reinvesting energy in other people and life.

MASKED GRIEF

With masked grief, a person may experience symptoms and problems but he or she does not connect them to their grief. They may have physical symptoms, pain and illness and sometimes these are related to the problems and illness of the deceased.

A visit to their physician might result in some understanding that their symptoms are linked to their grief.

Remember: The pace of recovery with normal grief is varied and individual. People will experience better times and worse times in the weeks and months after their loss. Most people can make a connection between their grief and their bodily distress, but some people cannot make this link.

EXAGGERATED GRIEF

In this case, grief reactions are greatly exaggerated. Sadness turns into severe depression and anxiety becomes a panic attack. The angry, bitter and guilty feelings may be the predominant feelings with few obvious feelings of sadness. Sometimes, a person's attempt to manage such overwhelming feelings results in self-destructive behaviour, such as excessive drinking and drug-taking.

People will always be changed in some way by their grief experience. For those who get 'stuck' in their unresolved grief – be it avoided, delayed, chronic or masked – it is important to seek help to address this complicated grief. If change and recovery are not happening over a period of time, it's possibly because the grief has become 'stuck' or complicated in some way.

RECOGNISING THE GOOD FROM THE BAD

In good grief-work, the process is long and the first three tasks of grieving, namely: accepting that the loss is a reality, entering into the emotions of grief, acquiring new skills, are done over and over again in various ways. The fourth task, reinvesting our energy in new ways, is achievable only after the first three tasks have been completed.

The way out of grief is through it. There are no short-cuts to life after loss.

The lyrics of an old spiritual reflect the essence of grief-work. Although not written specifically about grief, they capture the essential truths:

It's so high you can't get over it,
So low you can't get under it,
So wide you can't get around it,
You must go through the door.

PROMPT FOR YOUR PEN

Exercise	Reflection on your grief response

Reflect back on your losses and consider your responses to one or two major losses you've experienced:

• did you try to avoid any aspects of grief?
• did you try to get over it as quickly as possible?
• did you try to wait it out?

Have any of your grief responses led to your experiencing a form of complicated grief?

In recent years, some researchers have theorised that certain losses might be ambiguous losses and some grief might be disenfranchised grief.

AMBIGUOUS LOSS AND DISENFRANCHISED GRIEF

It feels like a loss, but is it really one? Sometimes we experience unclear losses as a response to a complicated situation. Whenever we feel a sense of grief, yet the ambiguity of the situation leaves us wondering what we are to do with our feelings. Ambiguous loss is the sort of loss that remains unverified by others, so there is little validation of what a person is experiencing and feeling.

Ambiguous loss remains unclear and indeterminate. As such it can be experienced as a devastating loss. An old nursery rhyme captures the distressing uncertainty of this sort of loss:

As I was walking up the stair,
I met a man who was not there.
He was not there again today.
Oh, how I wish he'd go away.

There is an absurdity and frustration in not being certain about a person's absence or presence. We all want certainty in our lives and those people living with ambiguous loss live with continuing doubt.

Ambiguous loss is confusing and people feel baffled and immobilised. They are trying to make sense of the situation. They are unsure as to whether the loss is permanent or temporary. If the sense of uncertainty continues, people sometimes respond in absolutes: either they act as if the person is completely gone, or deny that anything has changed.

There are two types of ambiguous loss. First, there is the situation in which people are perceived to be physically absent but psychologically present, because it is unclear whether they are dead or alive. Kidnapped children and missing soldiers illustrate this type of loss in its most dramatic form. More everyday examples include the losses within adoptive or divorced families where a parent or a child is seen as absent or missing. A second form of ambiguous loss occurs when a person is perceived as physically present but psychologically absent. This loss is seen in families where there is chronic mental illness of one member, or a severe addiction or Alzheimer's.

In a more dramatic form, it occurs when a person becomes comatose and on waking, is a different person. In a minor form, this type of ambiguous loss also occurs when people become excessively preoccupied with their work or other interests, to the exclusion of the important people in their lives.

Ambiguity complicates loss and complicates the grieving process. People can't start their grieving because the situation is indeterminate. The confusion freezes their grieving. The endless searching of a battlefield by the mother of a missing soldier, a wife's depression and withdrawal because her husband has suffered a brain injury and is no longer himself and the depressed husband of a woman with Alzheimer's, who no longer recognises him and their adult children, are all examples of the devastating effects of ambiguous loss.

There is no doubt that psychological absence can be equally devastating as physical absence. Yet, in cases of brain injury, stroke and Alzheimer's disease, the afflicted person is present, but his or her mind is not.

John Bayley, writing about his wife, the novelist Iris Murdoch, in **Elegy for Iris**, published in the **New Yorker**, put it succinctly, *'The Alzheimer's face indicates only an absence. It is, in the most literal sense, a mask.'*

Tessa, 39, summarises the dilemma for women like her who want to put some closure on their loss, but the absent person stays present:

> *'It's now 5 years since my mother knew me. It's been very frustrating, wanting to say goodbye to the her I once knew, but being left with this half-world feeling of saying goodbye without leaving.'*

All achievements are forgotten and all the faces of loved ones lost. Family members desperately cling to the barest threads of who their loved one once was.

Research has suggested that the more uncertain a family member is about their parent or partner's Alzheimer's status as absent of present, the greater the family member's vulnerability to depression. People who live with ambiguous loss describe themselves as living in a 'limbo world'.

Rabbi Earl A. Grollman in his book for caregivers of people with Alzheimer's re-emphasises the value of crying, *'The tight hard knot of suffering may be eased by the shedding of tears. Crying is an honest expression of grief that transcends words. Crying can release anxiety, dissolve tension, and help you confront your feelings more clearly.'*

Kenneth Doka introduced the concept of disenfranchised grief in his book: **Disenfranchised Grief: Recognizing the Hidden Sorrow.** Disenfranchised grief is grief experienced in circumstances where:

- the lost relationship is not socially recognised
- the grieving person is not recognised and supported
- the loss is not recognised

First, it is difficult to grieve openly for a lost relationship that is not socially recognised as legitimate. Great emphasis is placed on relationships by blood and marriage, yet there are many other relationships that are rewarding, often intense and important to people. Our friends, lovers, room-mates, caregivers, colleagues, teachers and foster parents may be just as important to us than more legitimate and formal family ties.

In the second situation, where the grieving person is not recognised and supported, we can nominate those people whom society does not view as experiencing grief or needing protection from grief. In the past, women who had miscarriages or agreed to adopt out their babies were not recognised as legitimate grievers who had suffered loss. Many such women experienced unresolved grief, for years, sometimes decades, because they were not socially permitted to feel and talk about their loss. Young children, people with intellectual disabilities and older people are sometimes not recognised in their loss, nor supported in their grief.

Thirdly, disenfranchised grief still is seen in the case of abortion, although it is less likely today to attach to a woman who has experienced a stillbirth. Older people again, with their associated losses of independence, freedom and self-esteem are often disenfranchised in their grief. The overwhelming losses associated with moving into a hostel or nursing home are not recognised fully. In some instances, disenfranchised grief is experienced by the immigrant, who despite their wish to migrate to a land offering greater opportunities, nevertheless might not be permitted to tell of the losses of the 'old country', and their grief in resettlement.

HOW TO TELL IF YOU NEED TO TURN BAD GRIEF INTO GOOD GRIEF

One of the hallmarks of normal or good grief is the way it heals itself. By doing good grief-work, the grieving person passes through the tasks of grieving in their own good time. After a time, a grieving person gradually is able to resume social functioning. Episodes of grief and sadness should be fewer and shorter and have less effect on the grieving person and their daily life. Episodes of disturbance decrease in number and length.

Good grief progresses, however erratically and episodically, towards recovery.

Professional help is needed should the grief process get fixated or stuck at any level. A warning sign might be if the person is unable to accept the reality of the death and continues to deny it, or when there is stalled healing with the person refusing to change things in recognition of their loss. Here we remember Queen Victoria, who kept a virtual shrine to Prince Albert. Another warning sign is where there is no real grieving. Where there is little emotional involvement, and hardly any emotion, even at the start, professional help is indicated.

Professional intervention is indicated to help turn bad grief into good grief whenever there is too much or too little grief or when the process starts and then stops, or in any grieving that isn't resolved in a time frame of approximately three years.

Failing to turn bad grief into good grief may well cost the person his or her chance for a renewed and fulfilled life.

THE TEST OF GOOD GRIEF

Only through the pain and torment can a grieving person find the road to recovery. The test of good grief is whether the person finally tolerates the bad times with passing pain and only faint sorrowful thoughts. Ideally, we should reach a point where we might feel nostalgic and have pleasant thoughts and be able to speak about our loss with honesty. We might speak affectionately of a lost loved one. The aching pain and distress have been transformed into nostalgia and passing sorrow. That is good grief.

8

MEN, WOMEN, CHILDREN AND GRIEVING

He shared their sorrow, and they became a part of his,
and the sharing spread their grief a little by thinning it.

MARJORIE KINNAN RAWLINGS [The Sojourner, 1953]

Men, women and children all walk together in their grief. Grief has no claim on gender or age. Men do grieve. Women do grieve. Children do grieve. There may be differences, and these differences may be real, or they may be perceived differences only. At times, they will be real differences. At other times, there will be only perceived differences. These perceived differences relate to grieving styles. Much of these differences are related to gender conditioning and stereotyping. Some of these differences are related to expectations concerning gender and age. Because grief affects us all, it is empowering to have more knowledge regarding how grief affects us differently, and how we might understand each other better – and help each other more.

GRIEF IS NOT GENDERED

Many books have been devoted to exploring the differences between men and women in their communication styles. Culturally dominant notions of masculinity and femininity are inculcated within us from infancy. In terms of grieving, it seems that there are differences between the genders. However, differences are just that – differences. Differences are neither right nor wrong, inferior nor superior neither good nor bad.

It sometimes seems that men and women are baffled by each other's ways of grieving. We might be moved to attempt to dictate how the other gender should grieve. Some women confide how upset they are by their partner's seeming lack of feelings. One woman, Ingrid, was very distraught by her husband's lack of language for grief in the face of the loss of their six-year-old child in a motoring accident. She said, *'My husband didn't have any words. I tried to believe he had feelings, but how could I understand what was going on for him when he had no words to describe his state. We'd just lost our son and he had no words.'*

Men, on the other hand, may be overwhelmed by women's ways of grieving. Some men have said how they have tired of the tears and crying and admonished their women for what to them appears to be continuing and self-inflicted pain. One couple who came to counselling after the cot death of their baby, played out this particular dynamic as a couple. As the woman and mother continued to tell and retell her tragedy, the man and father grew more and more impatient. In a confronting moment, some months after their loss he said, *'Don't think you've got the monopoly on grief. It's etched on my mind, and I think about him every day. But I can't give into it all the time. We have to accept the loss and get on with the business of living. There's no other way.'*

Perhaps some women yearn to have this apparent discipline, which allows men to separate and compartmentalise their lives. Men are seemingly better at distracting themselves from their grief in order to facilitate getting on with 'the business of living.'

While women might conclude that men are cold and heartless, men might conclude that women are too self-absorbed and emotional.

It's the old story of men intellectualising their feelings and women emoting theirs.

MEN, WOMEN AND THE LANGUAGE OF GRIEF

There might well be differences in the way we speak 'masculine' and 'feminine' language. Masculine language is essentially thought-focused, controlling, goal-oriented and concise. Feminine language, on the other hand, is essentially emotionally-focused, intuitive, elusive and fluid. From childhood, boys are taught to be interested in the external world, to be competitive, adventurous, independent, busy themselves with problem-solving tasks and to devalue, if not ignore, emotional issues. Conversely, girls are taught to be interested in others, to be co-operative, to be connected with others, to empathise with them, to be dependent, or perhaps interdependent, to be emotionally aware and to talk, talk and talk some more about their feelings.

Perhaps many men lack a language for grief. Perhaps this is what Ingrid meant when she said her husband had 'no words'.

However, just because men may not have the words, the language, to describe their pain, doesn't mean they don't have the feelings of pain. Researchers have found that when an emotion is felt, women are more likely, and more easily able to put a name to it. This is not surprising given that boys are told that tenderness, vulnerability and sensitivity are weaknesses for them. Bearing the mantle of masculinity means segmenting feelings and concealing them from view.

Elizabeth Levang in her book, **When Men Grieve**, writes,

> 'Grief comes to men like a live electric current. It's like plunging a fork in an electric toaster. The jolt is so jarring that men are forced, at least momentarily, to touch that deep, frightening void of numb and unspoken feelings. The discomfort is so immense, the man has no choice but to deal with it. Many believe they have amputated that part of themselves and so become confused and troubled. Still, many men are reluctant to risk being labeled a weeper or fool, and are embarrassed to show, let alone talk about, their emotions. You won't often see a man cry on someone's shoulder. Without the language of grief, a man will attempt to gloss over his feelings. In doing so, he will have no opportunity to reveal himself, thereby diminishing his capacity to heal.'

For many men, grief is something they need to problem-solve. Very rarely do women want to resolve their grief entirely on their own.

We live in a verbal society. Finding words to describe our feelings and our pain is vitally important for our healing. Sharing these words also is important. As Marjorie Kinnan Rawlings's quote at the beginning of this chapter suggests, sharing spreads and thins our sorrow.

TEARS ARE NOT GENDERED

Ann MacDonald, in her book, **Softly My Grief**, tells the story of her struggle to come to terms with grief. She confesses, *'The first time I saw a man cry I was shocked. The second time I was relieved...relieved to know that he could feel as I did and seek comfort in the release of tears.'*

These are telling words. They tell us about men and women – the differences and the similarities. They tell us about expectations – and reality. They imply that we live in a culture where we equate self-control with strength and maturity. Under pressure, strength lies in accepting yourself and your feelings – and the very normality of behaving like a human being – whatever gender you are. Crying is part of being a human being.

Self-control and strength are words often associated with maleness. One of the most potentially harmful messages most males grow up with is: *'Big boys don't cry'.*

Bob Deits, a pastoral counsellor and author writes in his book **Life After Loss**,

'Jack came to see me a few months after his wife died. He had been absent from church since her death. In the past, the two of them rarely missed a Sunday. He told me had had reached the church door several times, but just couldn't come in. He would begin to cry as the memories rushed over him of having Helen beside him and listening to her sing the hymns. Each time he tried to come in he would turn around and go home to cry alone. He didn't want anyone to see him 'being weak'.

As we talked, I discovered that he wasn't sleeping well and was eating infrequently. He was also having occasional chest pains and shortness of breath.

I told Jack that his unwillingness to cry was hurting him and blocking his ability to handle Helen's loss. It might sound unkind, but I scolded him for allowing his pride to keep him away from church and for his lack of confidence in the rest of us to be able to handle his grief.

I told him our church Cry Room at the back of the sanctuary was not only for parents with babies, but for adults who needed to cry and were uncomfortable crying in public. I also urged him to join the grief support group where he could talk and cry with other folks who would understand. Jack took me up on both suggestions.

Within a matter of weeks he was out of the Cry Room and back among the congregation. He began to sleep better and eat better. In time, his physical health returned to normal.'

Bob Deits believes in crying – for everyone. He has a sign in his office which reads: 'People and Tears are Welcome Here'.

Rabbi Earl A. Grollman again shares some words of potential liberation, *'Unfortunately, our society places restrictions on who may choose to cry. Too often, crying is permissible for women and children, but not for men. "Don't be a sissy. Big boys don't cry." "Take it like a man." Familiar messages like these have made many men consider tears a sign of weakness, of failure, of vulnerability, of lost control.'*

PROMPT FOR YOUR PEN

Exercise   Expectations of men

Answer True or False to the following statements:
- men do not feel as much as women
- mothers are closer to their children than are fathers
- hugging is a good way for men to show their feelings
- it is okay for men to be upset and to cry
- men generally get over grief before women
- it helps men to recover from grief by going back to work quickly

Look at your responses. What have you learned about your attitudes to men and their expressions of feelings?

Adapted from McBride, 1996

MEN AND GRIEF

Through their conditioning and society's expectations, men's ways of coping may be opposed to what is thought to be the normal requirements for grieving a loss. Men are not usually expected to:

- lose control over themselves
- lose control over the situation
- be dependent
- show fear
- express sadness
- be passive
- be anxious and insecure

Often even very young boys will be told at funerals, *'be strong'* and to *'take good care of mummy and your sisters'*.

Men will generally be greeted – by both men and women – with questions that distance their grief. They might be asked: *'How are the children?'* or *'How's your wife coping?'* These questions avoid having to ask the men how they are feeling. They are partly protective of the men – and partly protective of the person asking the question. These questions are predicated on unwritten societal rules that say we must not ask embarrassing questions of men for fear they will break down. We might fear the consequence perhaps of once men beginning to let their feelings out, they might not be able to shut them off. Of course, women might also fear this of themselves. However, men are more inclined to view emotions as volatile and uncontrollable, so it's safer to keep such feelings concealed. Because men are given such little encouragement to express their emotions, not surprisingly, they are hesitant to expose any emotional vulnerability.

One theory suggests that men have six main ways of coping with their grief:

- to remain silent and not to talk about feelings
- to grieve secretly, for example, at the graveside alone
- to take physical or other action, for example, to fix things or take legal action or to punish the cause of their difficulties
- to express anger instead of yearning, sadness and despair
- to become immersed in activity, for example, to return to work quickly
- to use alcohol and drugs

Of course, some women also might respond in some of these ways, but there are more men who act in such a stereotypical way in response to societal pressures on them as men to be 'strong'. In fact, some of these coping styles may be beneficial – for a while. You might remember that activity can help use up the adrenaline in the body and thereby control stress. It is only by examining these responses carefully that we can determine whether men are reacting in ways that are useful or not.

THERE ARE ALWAYS EXCEPTIONS TO THE RULE

Before deciding that men and women have absolute grieving styles, it's important to consider the exceptions. We all know men who are sensitive,caring and empathic and we all know women who are distant, task-focused and non-empathic. As human beings, men and women share like qualities, and the apparent polarisation that takes place between us may sometimes be more apparent than real.

John Bramblett in his book ***When Goodbye is Forever***, describes the differences in response by his wife and him to the death of their youngest son. He writes,

'In the early weeks following Christopher's death, both Mairi and I saw that we were dealing with our tragedy very differently. For the first time in our married life, we were unable to accommodate each other because we were trying to deal successfully with our own individual needs.

Mairi is by nature a very private person. I am an extrovert. With Christopher's death, Mairi's need for privacy deepened and my extroverted nature became more exaggerated. The feelings and experiences I chose to impart to friends were to Mairi very private and personal matters....

I knew what she was thinking; she knew what I was talking about. I wanted to communicate my experience: it was part of my way of coping. She felt that talking about those striking episodes in our family's life cheapened them. She recognized how special they were, and her private nature conflicted with my openness about them. Neither of us was wrong; our approaches were just different.'

In John Bramblett's situation, the accepted stereotypes of male and female grieving were reversed. For Mairi and John Bramblett, their communication styles and individual needs temporarily interfered with their relationship. Neither could understand totally how the other could behave the way they did.

Following the death of a child, growing alienation between parents is a common occurrence. Statistics reveal that within one year of the death of a child, 75% of the affected marriages are in serious trouble. Of these, a high proportion end up in divorce. For Mairi and John Bramblett, the challenge became how they could work together in their grief and commit to their union and support each other through the difficult times.

John Bramblett writes that through their love they survived and *'...in this process we learned a great deal about a deeper form of love – one that "bears all things, endures all things."'*

WOMEN HELPING MEN WITH GRIEF

Women can help the men in their lives by understanding that, generally speaking, although they both grieve losses, men and women do have a different language for grief. Encouraging men to understand how traditional male behaviour might impede their grieving is important. So is the encouragement of men in seeking medical assistance should they experience physical reactions to grief and develop illness. In our society, women rather than men are more likely to seek medical attention. Men might be encouraged to express the full range of grief emotions, not just anger, but sadness, guilt, frustration, helplessness and vulnerability. Women might work with men to help them communicate their thoughts and feelings more freely. This involves women reaching out and remaining empathic, even in the face of initial denial and anger by men not wanting to appear vulnerable. Men might be encouraged to use tears to release emotions. Tears should be seen as therapeutic and a helpful release.

MEN AND WOMEN UNDERSTANDING ONE ANOTHER

Grieving couples need to reach their own unique set of arrangements. There are no absolute guidelines or rules. However, it is crucial that the couple develop good communication skills and practise respectful listening. Listening, supporting, comforting and empathising are skills needed by both the man and the woman in the face of grief, when they feel their life has abruptly gone out of control. Displacing anger on one another, finding fault and apportioning blame may have temporary benefits in relieving the tension and stress of grief, but such behaviours are unlikely to forge a good relationship at a time it is most needed.

Bad things won't stop happening just because we think they should. People for whom we care and those we love dearly will get hurt and our heartache can be overwhelming. To survive as a couple takes determination and great skill. To survive together takes a joint effort. Sometimes it takes an effort of gigantic proportions. Finding inner strength in the depths of your soul and sharing this with your partner is a good beginning. It takes strength, courage and commitment to the relationship to walk together in sorrow.

THE GRIEFS OF CHILDREN

Let's take a trip back in the time machine. Imagine what it's like to be a child again. Remember how small you felt? How vulnerable? How powerless? How insecure? Remember when you didn't have the words to express what you felt?

Knowing what you know now as an adult, it's hard to believe you once felt so limited in your existence. However, by reminding yourself that children are children, and not 'miniature adults', you'll have more awareness of how big a hurt grief can be for little people.

Whatever the nature of the loss, major or minor, of objects or people, you'll have some idea of how children grieve if you remember the following four points:

- children have all the sadness, fear, anger, guilt and other emotions that adults have
- children have limited exposure to life and less understanding of what is happening to them than adults have
- children might assume more readily they are to blame for what happened in some way, than adults routinely do
- children do not have the vocabulary that adults have, to express the way they are feeling.

GOOD POLICY AND PRACTICE WITH CHILDREN

As adults, we play a major role in the future lives of children after they experience a loss. It's good policy and practice for adults to assume responsibility for explaining, clearly and directly, to children the loss they have experienced. When adults attempt to protect and shield children from their experience, the children turn to their imaginations and the imagined loss experience may become worse than the real one.

Guilt is a common experience for children. They remember feeling guilty and being blamed for broken toys and messy bedrooms. Children easily might interpret the adult's silence and sadness as disappointment in them. They have to be reassured that the loss had nothing to do with their behaviour.

Adults need to respond in ways that help the child face loss and to work through grief in their own way, much as we must do. If adults assume that responsibility for helping their children, and sometimes that means getting professional help, then the children will heal and there will be no lasting emotional scars.

TELLING CHILDREN ABOUT DEATH

The old nursery rhyme,

"Doctor, Doctor, will I die?
Yes, my child, as so shall I"

illustrates how frank and open people were in talking about death – otherwise it would not have been written. However, times have changed and euphemisms now are commonly used, so that people, 'go away on a long trip', 'fall asleep and not wake up', 'be taken up to Heaven with God' and 'pass away'.

Adults shielding children from death, being sent away in times of critical illness and being prevented from attending funerals and told that 'Grandma went on a long journey' have become common scenarios. In earlier times, before modern medicine was able to fight and control disease, fatal illness and the facts of grief were everyday experiences. Children, from a young age, became aware of the naturalness of the cycle of life – of ageing, illness and death. Children, along with other family members, gathered when a death occurred. Children were able to experience tears along with their parents and realise the impact of loss on family members. Death was not a mystery to the child. It is thought that this exposure and experience of loss from a young age helped children develop coping patterns for future experiences.

Today, when many elderly relatives are placed in institutions, such as hospitals and nursing homes, children do not have the opportunity to see the person grow old, become ill and eventually die. Some of these changes can affect the way children experience death – and how they might respond to it. Some researchers have found that the adult's response further can complicate the child's understanding. Parents often tell themselves that the fact of death is beyond the child's comprehension. They tell themselves that they want to protect the child from the anguish they themselves are experiencing. Yet, when a major loss, like a death occurs, the child senses from the reaction of those around him or her that something significant has happened. But the child often does not know what.

Some studies have demonstrated that adults prefer to distract children from the topic of death and to deny that the children are upset. Yet, the children *are* upset. Are these adults protecting their children or themselves? In one study, some parents were confronted with their dilemma and admitted that they avoided the topic of grief because they could not face the intensity of the children's feelings. This seemingly protective attitude can lead to a child's confusion, feelings of betrayal, a sense of breached trust and perhaps an unwillingness to accept the fact of death and to grieve it.

The desire by many adults to 'spare' children is often caused by their own feelings of discomfort, fear and anxiety. Others believe children are too immature to be capable of experiencing the full range of feelings at a time of loss. Such rationalisations leave the child vulnerable to not knowing the facts and being confused about their feelings and responses.

Childhood is a special time of life. It is a time of life when children should be supported and encouraged by all their caregivers to discover facts about the world and to locate themselves in that world.

Researchers and counsellors report that the most important influence on how children react at the time of a death experience is the response of parents and other significant people in the child's life.

TALKING TO CHILDREN

In talking to children about death, we are forced to look at ourselves – we have to answer questions and be ready to speak about what we ourselves believe. Do we, as adults, know what children think and believe about death?

There is research evidence to suggest even very young children can recognise the differences between 'dead' and 'living'. For instance, an 18-months-old child on seeing a dead bird can recognise it as dead. However, it is some years before a child appears to recognise that the death of a person is permanent.

Some adults are gifted in engaging with and talking to children. But all parents can raise the subject of death as part of teaching children about life and the world in which they live. The death of a pet, a dead bird by the side of the road, an ambulance speeding down the street to a motor car accident, the prolong illness of an elderly relative – these are all instances that provide opportunities for discussions between adults and children.

Some guidelines for helping children in their understanding follow.

GUIDELINES FOR HELPING CHILDREN UNDERSTAND

Provide an open and honest atmosphere

Do everything possible to provide an atmosphere in which it is easy for children to ask questions and express their thoughts and feelings. For example, it may be important to sit on the floor with the child or to hold them in your lap to give them a sense of security and to allay any fears they might have. You might consider involving the child in family discussions about the person, their death and the funeral plans.

An important point to remember: adults internalise their feelings while children act them out. Watch out for signs of distress that tell you the child needs your attention.

Try to understand how the child interprets their experience of death

Ask the child specific questions which enables them to tell you what they are thinking, for example,

- have you ever seen a dead person?
- have you ever been to a funeral? What was it like?
- what would you like to know?

It's important to be willing to speak matter-of-factly with the child. He or she will find that reassuring. Sit at their height with them, on the floor or at a low table.

Providing children with pens, crayons, paper, colouring books and modelling clay is helpful because it enables them to express themselves non-verbally.

Try to give correct and factual information as simply as you can

In giving the facts simply you can dispel myths and fears of the child's imagination. Don't use expressions such as 'Mummy is sleeping' and

'Grandpa has gone away', because young children take your words as literal fact. Children may interpret the statement that grandpa has 'gone away' to mean that grandpa wanted to leave them. By using euphemisms such as a person is 'sleeping', you might create an situation where the child waits for the deceased to 'wake up'. If the child does not perceive death to be a permanent condition, it may be helpful to repeat a simple statement to reinforce this fact.

Perhaps a statement like: 'Remember (name) has died and when a person dies, it means their body no longer works. Their heart stops and they don't breathe anymore. They don't have to eat, drink or sleep. They never get too hot or too cold. Nothing hurts them anymore. They don't need their body anymore. That means we won't see (name) again.'

Try to provide some way for the child to say good-bye

Perhaps the child can draw a picture to be placed in the casket. It's important to make a copy for the child to keep. Maybe the child can write a note or make a cassette-taped message to farewell their important person.

AGE CAN MAKE A DIFFERENCE

Children grieve and express their feelings differently according to age and their developmental level. Loss and grief are part of daily life from infancy onwards.

One mother, Roberta, recounted her experience of her very young child suffering grief, which at the time was not recognised. Her 14-month-old son showed marked changes in behaviour when his six week old brother died from cot death. Her son became tearful and irritable and aggressive when playing with his friends. It was only weeks later that Roberta began to realise the link between her son's acting out behaviour and the cot death of her baby. Perhaps some of her son's response was because he sensed Roberta's sadness and tensions. However, as Roberta says,

> *'I was stunned when 19 months later, I brought his new brother*
> *home from the hospital. My son, just out of the blue, asked,*
> *'Will this baby die too, mummy?''*

Her son's awareness of what had happened was demonstrated clearly. Roberta said that they have never 'openly' talked about the cot death.

Remember, infants require attachment, physical touch and stroking for their development. They show an understanding of loss well before their first birthday. A fear of separation begins at about this time.

To the age of about four, children sense loss and sadness, but cannot conceptualise death as permanent. From the ages of 5 to 9, understanding death becomes clear to most children. They realise that pets and people die and that death is final. By the adolescent years, the child has an individual and social dimension understanding of death. They know they live in a particular social context and that there are consequences for them and their family.

It has been found that the death of a same-gender parent when the child is 12 or 13, seems to have the potential for long-term problems. Consequently, it might be wise to seek professional assistance in this case.

As young people reach late adolescence, they raise philosophical questions about the meaning of life. This is a time of energy and exuberance and many late adolescents feel immortal. Death, if it visits, is an intrusion in their reality and experienced as very painful. Should one of their peers die, their sense of security is challenged tremendously. If that death was a suicide, the adolescent may become moody and demonstrate impulsive or risk-taking behaviour. The adolescent in this situation should be encouraged to attend a grief support group or counselling sessions.

WHEN CHILDREN DON'T HAVE THE WORDS

Grieving children sometimes cannot express and explore their feelings. This may be because they are too young and don't yet have the words, or because their explosive feelings frighten them too much to put into words.

Play and art work allow for the safe and 'acceptable' expression of explosive feelings.

Children are able to express symbolically what they cannot put into words. By letting children draw, paint and play, they may regain a sense of the self-control that was lost when they experienced a sense of loss over significant events in their lives.

Art was the medium that helped seven-year-old Joanna express her trauma and grief. Joanna's mother had made lunch for Joanna and her friend and told them to go and play in the rumpus room. Joanna's mother then went into the living room and shot herself. Joanna and her friend found her.

Joanna's father took her to therapy where she sat drawing pictures of her mummy. Some of these pictures were angry, others fearful, and still others, sad. There was one picture which was happy. These pictures reflected the range of feelings Joanna felt. When she was asked to describe her art work, she confirmed that she was upset her mum had left her and she felt afraid she was to blame. She said she felt sad mummy was no longer alive, but she could remember times when mummy had been happy. Children like Joanna need professional help and they need to be reassured that their parent didn't die because she was angry with them and they shouldn't blame themselves.

Perhaps the most startling example of the power of art therapy for children is the case of a five-year-old child who was dying of a rare cardiac condition brought on by a virus. Her family were unsure as to her awareness of her impending death. However, all their uncertainty dissipated when their little girl, with a therapist, did a drawing of her family. She drew a tree with six branches, each with a red heart at the end of the branch and one branch for each family member – her parents and four siblings. She drew no branch for herself. On the ground, beneath the tree, she had drawn a large red heart representing herself. Her surprised parents confirmed that the little girl was not aware that her heart was the cause of her illness and they were even more surprised that she instinctively knew the truth of her condition.

A FINAL NOTE

To fully understand the griefs of children is almost impossible for an adult. We can enter into some of their sadness by being attuned to apparently irrelevant behaviour and understanding the child's needs to act out. Accepting the naughtiness as a normal protest against the child's loss of security, loss of friendship, loss of love, loss of a home, loss of the parents' relationship and all other losses is important if we are to validate children in their experience. The myriad of losses a child may experience all have implications in the child's life. As adults we must try to be empathic with the enormity of the loss for the child. Even if we judge the loss to be trivial, we must try to understand its impact on the child. Remember, the most important influence on how children react to loss is the response of the adults around them.

9

GETTING OVER GRIEVING

What was so terrible about grief was not grief itself,
but that one got over it.

P. D. JAMES [Innocent Blood, 1980]

Perhaps as P. D. James suggests, it is shocking to think that we have gotten over grief. However, we must realise that if we are to get on with a productive life, then getting over grieving is our responsibility – to others and ourselves. Recovering – getting over grieving – is not easy. We have seen how painful grief-work can be.

ACKNOWLEDGING YOUR LOSS

Acknowledging a loss is the most important step in your recovery. By acknowledging your loss you begin to take charge of your life and full responsibility for your feelings.

Emotional pain is a sign of progress towards a new reality. It is important to understand – and remind yourself – that you will not always feel as you do at this moment. Your journey towards recovery lies through the pain of the acknowledgement of the loss.

You will tell your story of your loss again and again. Sometimes you'll find that others have finished listening long before you've finished with your need to talk. Some of your friends will compliment you – and reward you – with kind words and more frequent visits if you pretend to be on top of things. If you understand that such tensions are common, then you can be more patient – and forgiving – of others and yourself.

C. S. Lewis wrote about this feeling of others' embarrassment and its effects on the grieving person in **A Grief Observed**,

> *'An odd by-product of my loss is that I'm aware of being an embarrassment to anyone I meet. At work, in the street, I see people, as they approach me, trying to make up their minds whether they'll say 'something about it' or not. Some funk it altogether. I like best the well brought up young men, almost boys, who walk up to me as if I were a dentist, turn very red, get it over, and then edge away to the bar as quickly as they decently can. Perhaps the bereaved ought to be in special settlements like lepers.'*

People will want you to start living 'normally' long before you are ready to do so. Almost every divorced person or widow or widower , at some time, will hate the question: 'How are you?' because they have discovered that it can be a cue to say 'Fine, thank you' regardless of how miserable they might really feel. 'Fine, thank you' seems to be the only acceptable answer.

Stories abound about divorced men and women finding friends taking sides and making judgements at the very time these people need a friendly ear. Some widows talk about rejection at social gatherings – the bridge club, at tennis – where they were welcome before – as a couple. Alternatively, some younger widows report men, whom they consider friends, making sexual advances. Anger and confusion are common responses on the woman's behalf. In their vulnerable state, they might feel less than flattered. What they need is friendship, not sexual exploitation.

Margaret Mead, the celebrated anthropologist and feminist, said,

> *'When a person is born we celebrate, when they marry we are jubilant, when they die we act as if nothing has happened.'*

The reason for these reactions appears to be the balance of joyful gain. Birth and marriage represent loss – but also positive gains. Most people know what to say and how to behave in these circumstances. However, we see death as cancelling out joy and consequently, we don't know what to say to the grieving person. We might feel very uncomfortable in the presence of someone else's grief – and we might feel helpless. We might feel too uncomfortable to reach out to the grieving person.

WITH A LITTLE HELP FROM SOME FRIENDS

There is no doubt that having some good friends can be important when you are struggling with an array of ever-changing and bewildering emotional states, in the landscape of grief.

It is at this time that we need a safe place to be and to feel safe with people whom we know and trust. We need people who can provide us with security in our turmoil and acceptance in our distress. We need a place where we are permitted to acknowledge if necessary, our sad feelings – and still feel as if we are accepted.

Sadly, not all our friends can supply us with the necessary security and care we need after a major loss. Some people describe the support and care they received from friends as wonderful, yet others experience confusion and a sense of being let down by friends who appear to be unwilling or unable to offer them support, care, or even friendship in their grief.

Maria McCarthy, the woman who was hit by a car while jogging described how she was intrigued by other people's responses. Some friends couldn't do enough, while others could not even seem to acknowledge that she had suffered a major life set-back and loss. She said, *'My vulnerability brought out other people's vulnerability. Some people didn't want me to grieve or to be depressed. But I had to tell people I needed to do that to get on with it... It was a burden, I didn't want to be nice, to smile, when I didn't feel like it.'*

We can feel a tremendous sense of betrayal when friends fail to accept and acknowledge us in our grief. We might think that's what friends are for and puzzle over how they could do this to us.

We might do well to remember that someone is bound to say something that can only be called 'cruel'. However, we might reconsider this judgement and realise that some people may say careless things sometimes.

Susan, who spoke before of the trauma of her rape, experienced such a careless comment from her male boss. Although he had been supportive and sensitive, he blurted out 'I suppose you feel you've got 'rape victim' tatooed on your forehead' when a group of her colleagues were having lunch about three weeks after the rape. Susan said his comment met with dead silence and then she decided he hadn't meant it in a malicious way. She says,

> 'After my initial surprise, I laughed it off because he looked so ashen and shocked himself after he'd said it. I think he'd meant it humourously, but no-one laughed until I did. Then it was like a nervous laugh. I figured it was his way of saying something but he didn't know how to say it.'

Perhaps even more hurtful than careless things people say are the times when we yearn for some words of acknowledgement of our loss and pain and we hear silence. It might feel that there is a conspiracy of silence around us whenever we are present. Again, it's useful to remind ourselves that this silence means our friends and colleagues don't know what to say.

SOME FRIENDS DON'T KNOW HOW TO HELP

Some friends may want to help, but be limited by knowing how they can help. They might worry that they'll say the wrong thing and upset us. Should they invite us out a week after we've suffered a loss or not? If they do, will we consider it insensitive? If they don't, will their silence and lack of invitation mean we will think they have excluded and forgotten us? If we are invited to a party, will the fun and laughter upset us enough for us to leave early and leave our friends feeling guilty?

There are bound to be some misunderstandings and mistakes made when we might be confused and only have a hazy idea ourselves of what we want in the first few weeks after a loss.

The best way to find out what a grieving person wants and needs is simply to ask them. It is best to be honest. We need to tell our friends we might not be ready to mix socially at a party, or that we had to leave early because we were troubled by memories and needed to be alone with our thoughts and feelings. We owe it to our friends to let them know that sometimes we need to talk and talk about our feelings and fears, hopes and dreams, and that at other times, we need to withdraw.

Of course, we also need to recognise that because of our grief, we are not capable of being a very good, caring friend to anyone for a while. When we are grieving, it's difficult to be empathic with the many things that are absorbing our friends in their lives. Friends who are sensitive and empathic will understand that we are undergoing changes and challenges and that our world has been shattered. However, they still might not be sure of how to help us. Should they continue to relate to us 'normally' or should they censure what they say? For example, if we lost a mother, would it be insensitive of them to mention their mother to us? Should they mention someone we've lost by name?

It's important to remember that there is no absolute right or wrong way to behave. The rules depend on the individuals involved in the interaction. A major loss will affect a friendship in so far as both sides need to be willing to be patient, to listen and learn from each other.

One thing is for certain. It is the people, the friends who stand by you in your struggle with grief who are likely to be genuine friends for life. Because they have been a part of your experience, their lives too will be changed.

FAIR-WEATHER FRIENDS

Perhaps you'll find that you have good-time friends who are just that – people with whom you can have a good time. However, these friends are not long-term friends who have become part of our history. They are the people we can escape with to enjoy ourselves, but not necessarily people with whom we share our deepest feelings. Don't expect these people to support you in your grief – but you might be content to have them in the periphery of your life – to have a good time with when you're ready to have a good time.

WHAT HELPS US

- knowing people who care about us
- having someone to listen to us when we need to talk
- knowing we don't have to talk if we don't want to
- to learn about grief from other people's experiences
- to read about grief and understand it better

WHAT DOESN'T HELP US

- to be told we'll get over it in time
- to be told to pull ourselves together
- to be told things could be worse
- to be told it was for the best
- to be ignored by friends
- for people to pretend that nothing has happened

Grace Noll Crowell expressed the value of supportive friends and the hope that emerges from their interactions with us in **To One in Sorrow** from **Songs of Hope**:

> *Let me come in where you are weeping,*
> *friend,*
> *And let me take your hand.*
> *I who have known a sorrow such as*
> *yours,*
> *can understand.*
> *Let me come in. I would be very still*
> *beside you in your grief,*
> *I would not bid you cease your weeping,*
> *friend,*
> *Tears bring relief.*
> *Let me come in – I would only breathe a*
> *prayer,*
> *And hold your hand,*
> *For I have known a sorrow such as yours,*
> *And understand.*

HELP FROM OTHERS

For many people, grief-work is not done alone – not absolutely alone. We are alone in our grief, but it can help to talk to someone who has experienced a loss similar to our own. These people are like us, but different.

We must remember that no two people will grieve in exactly the same way – not even two people in the same family. Often, the circumstances are similar, but the details offer differences between our loss and theirs.

Support groups enable those people going through similar losses to get in touch with one another. These groups provide support and encouragement to talk about our loss. These groups also provide special knowledge and understanding of the emotions generated by a particular kind of loss. Many people say that joining such a support group helps them to know someone has actually survived a similar loss.

For other people, seeking professional counselling help is the answer. This counselling help may be one-to-one or family grief counselling – if that is appropriate.

Counsellors are trained to listen carefully and to help the client express his or her thoughts and feelings in a safe environment. In providing these conditions, the client is enabled to work through their issues and reach their own decisions.

The unique properties of the counsellor-client relationship create a sense of safety for the client. This safety is created by the limitations of the relationship. The counsellor is not a friend. Consequently, no friendship is lost by whatever is said – or left unsaid. There is no need to expect equality in the relationship – the client is permitted to be as 'self-centred' as they need to be. The client is not expected to, nor should they have to, listen to the counsellor's description of their own hard times. Some sharing is appropriate, this is called 'self-disclosure'. However, self-disclosure on behalf of the counsellor is only appropriate where it facilitates further understanding and insight for the client. The counselling sessions are for the client – and should rightly focus on the client.

At its essence, counselling offers a grieving person time to talk about difficult feelings in a safe place with a skilled listener.

OPENING NEW DOORS

You reach the point where you realise that it's time to move on and get on with life. Yet, it seems difficult, sometimes impossible, to make a decision.

But in order to recover your balance after a major loss, you need to make a decision to let go of your grief.

You need to leave the room of your past and open the new door to the room of your future. This future is a new and different one. The choice is a scary one, but your recovery dictates you choose to move forward.

IT'S TIME TO CHOOSE

There comes a time – and you will recognise it – in your grief-work when you need to make a choice.

Rabbi Earl Grollman in his book, **Time Remembered** says,

'It's a risk to attempt new beginnings...Yet the greater risk is for you to risk nothing. For there will be no further possibilities of learning and changing, of travelling upon the journey of life...You were strong to hold on. You will be stronger to go forward to new beginnings.'

Moving forward to new beginnings means setting goals for yourself.

PROMPT FOR YOUR PEN

Exercise	Setting goals

Ask yourself the following questions and record them in your journal:

- what tasks do I need to complete in the next seven days?
- what barriers keep me from doing what I want to do?
- what resources do I have to overcome these barriers?
- what help do I need to do the things I want to do?
- what spiritual resources do I have – or need to find – to help me get on with my life?
- what things would I like to do in the next three months?
- What would my life look like in one year if I could have my way?

Now, choose one goal from your seven day, three month and one year list. Write down each of the goals.
Finally, the challenge:
Indicate how you will know when you have reached each of them.

This setting of short, medium and long-term goals for yourself will begin to open doors for your future and help you get over your grief. Don't be too hard on yourself. You may not reach all your goals. That doesn't matter. What matters is: you are beginning to make choices for your life after loss.

FOSTERING HOPE

Despair threatens our very existence. Yet feelings of despair can be very strong, often overwhelming, during your grief-work. Despair saps us of energy and the hopelessness we feel immobilises us. Rather than giving in to despair, we need to work hard to nurture new opportunities and new dreams.

We need to work hard to see the positive things in life – satisfaction, pleasure and beauty. We all can feel good about something – however small or trivial it might seem. We need to look inward to find the strengths we possess, look around us for the support we have and cling to the vestiges of our faith in the future.

Hope. Hope is important. Hope sustains us. Hope can motivate us when we might otherwise feel immobilised. Hope is what finally pushes us to re-engage freely with life.

Hope illuminates all the possibilities in life. Hope encourages us to expand our understanding of ourselves and our place in the world.

Finding hope is not easy after a major loss. But it is imperative that we find hope. Hope is essential to our healing.

In the words of Samuel Smiles, *'Hope is like the sun, which, as we journey towards it, casts the shadow of our burden behind us.'*

LETTING GO OF GRIEF

Grief begins with a terrible loss. Grief has changed you but it hasn't destroyed you. You know that grief is a powerful teacher.

You are different now. You may be looking into your own beliefs with new eyes, what may have been significant before may now appear trivial. You may set new priorities and redefine your needs. You are growing emotionally and spiritually by knowing that pain need not last forever and you can cherish your memories and look forward to a new opportunities in the future.

Alice in Lewis Carroll's **Alice's Adventures in Wonderland**, captures the value of change in our lives:

> "Who are You?" said the Caterpillar. Alice replied, rather
> shyly, "I hardly know, Sir, just at present – at least I know
> who I **was** when I got up this morning, but I think I must have
> been changed several times since then."

Like Alice, you have made changes to adjust to your loss and to recover your claim on life.

The end of grief is not despair and emptiness. There is a beginning, middle and end to our grief. Grieving means coming to accept what has happened in our lives. Letting go of the grief means recovery and looking forward to the potential life holds. Letting go means finding a new you.

———————

10

LESSONS OF LOSS

To live is to suffer, to survive is to find meaning in the suffering.

GORDON ALLPORT

Gordon Allport's quote rings true for many people who have suffered – and found meaning in that suffering. Perhaps this meaning has not been gained immediately, although for some people, there are urgent insights as a consequence of their grief experience. For others, the lessons of loss and the meaning which they interpret comes later.

In an earlier quote by George Sand it was suggested that grief is as much about finding as it is about losing. George Sand might be right. Grief is about recovering your balance after loss. Grief is about enduring the stresses and challenges of grief-work and recovery is linked to the discipline of doing your grief-work.

Doing grief-work adds a valuable new dimension to your life. You will emerge from your grief-work stronger and more compassionate than you were before.

Sarah, a 27-year-old woman who was raped and left for dead, tells of a long and painful process of recovery. Her assailant had jumped her from behind and beat her with his fist and a rock before sexually assaulting her and then repeatedly choked her until she passed out. Her ordeal involved not only a brutal physical attack, but also the humiliation of having to obey his sadistic orders. She was so visibly injured when she was found that she believes she was 'spared the insult of disbelief and blame' by police and medical personnel. Over the next few months, Sarah's sense of outrage at the injustice done to her alternated with debilitating depression. She joined a rape survivors' support group and went into therapy. She took self-defence classes and became active as a speaker in forums against sexual violence. She slowly began her grieving for her psychological losses and resumed her life.

However, as Sarah tells it, her life was a changed one – a paradoxical life. She felt stronger than ever before, and more vulnerable. She felt more determined to change the world, but in need of withdrawal from that world. Eventually, she reached the point where she realised her recovery meant incorporating the awful experience into her life and carrying on – knowing that the rape had happened and she was no longer a victim. She says,

> *I remember the group leader in the support group saying at our first meeting that 'you will never be the same but you can be better'. Slowly, I began to understand. When your life is shattered, you are forced to pick up the pieces and you have a chance to stop and examine them. It's then that you have a chance to say, 'I think I'll work on that' or 'I don't want this anymore.' In some ways, I've had to give up a lot, but I've also gained new insights and skills and I no longer feel a victim. I believe it's an honour being a survivor – it's an accomplishment, and although I won't put it on my CV, I'm proud of it.'*

Sarah's comment highlights the idea that from adversity and loss comes positive change. Picking up the pieces of her life allowed her the time to re-examine that life and develop new understandings.

ILLNESS AND GRIEF TRANSFORMING THE SELF

An illness and the grief that follows becomes special – even precious – for some people. They see it as a path to self-knowledge. As people are challenged to redefine themselves, they uncover aspects of themselves they did not know existed. James suffered a stroke at 55 and successfully rehabilitated himself. He believes,

> *The illness and all the grief I experienced meant I made discoveries about myself. The experience was so intense and I found I was so alert to things when I was recovering. It was like I had an increased sensitivity. I wouldn't*

trade that time for anything. It was tough but dealing with it made me the person I am today. I believe I'm a better person for that stroke. I'm far more understanding, patient and immediate in what I do. I can't let the time slip away – if I want to do something, the illness taught me I shouldn't put it on hold. Rejoice and enjoy the time you have – it's so precious.'

Robert McCrum, after his experience of the losses of having a stroke at 42 writes,

'Sometimes I think perhaps I am dreaming. Occasionally, I even say out loud: 'Am I dreaming? Did this really happen?' But no, I am not dreaming. Even though I am much better now, I am changed forever.'

LOSS INTO GAIN

The theme of gaining something positive after loss recurs time and again. People who have experienced loss and grieved, their counsellors and researchers all mention the possibility of growth and resilience following loss. Some people feel they learn something about themselves and others after a loss.

We must be careful not to be facile about this. Simply by asking the question: 'Have you found anything positive in the experience of loss' of some people may well receive the resounding response: 'Hell, no'. It can be a matter of timing. Sometimes the gains of loss are discovered much later. One study found that even one month after a major loss, 73% of people said they had found something positive in their loss experience and by 18 months after their loss, 81% said they had found something positive in their experience.

There is no doubt that a traumatic event, such as a major loss, can create developmental changes in people by confronting them with new situations and issues. Observing yourself doing things you never thought you could do certainly can lead to growth and change in your self-perception.

Loss and the grieving that follow can teach us a lot. If we have done our good grief-work, we might well believe our loss has become gain and our pain resulted in growth.

LESSONS OF LOSS

Lesson 1: The value of living in the present

Grief teaches us the importance of living in the present. After a major loss, we realise the value of every precious moment. When we are willing to live 'in the present' then we can find hidden treasures everywhere. Just think of the beautiful colours of a summer sunrise, a flower in full bloom or the excited expression on a child's face as a kite ascends. Many people plan and search, yet never find such treasures. By being willing to live in the present moment, we allow ourselves to experience their wonder.

Maria McCarthy says,

'I've been given a gift to repair myself and I feel I owe somebody. I want to savour every minute.'

Like Maria, many people speak about their gratitude for each day. Gabrielle, 30, is a survivor of incest. Her sexual abuse by her father began when she was nine. At 17, she took him to court and he was charged – but only with those episodes of abuse that Gabrielle had recorded. When she sought help at 16 from a counsellor, she had been told she must have dates and instances of abuse. She now laughs and says, *'I'd have kept a logbook if I'd known.'* Thirteen years later, after a lot of grief-work, in individual counselling and support groups, she says,

'Ever since that court hearing, I have lived for each day. When I heard the words, 'Please remove the prisoner', I knew I could start my life. But it took years to really emotionally start living. Now, I'm married and I have a lovely little girl and I have so much going for me. I bless each day.'

Carpe Diem by Horace captures the spirit of living in the present – it celebrates 'seizing the day':

Don't ask (we may not know), Leuconoe,
What the gods plan for you and me.
Leave the Chaldees to parse
The sentence of the stars.

Better to bear the outcome, good or bad,
Whether Jove purposes to add
Fresh winters to the past
Or to make this the last

Which now tires out the Tuscan sea and mocks
Its strength with barricades of rocks.
Be wise, strain clear the wine
And prune the rambling vine

Of expectation. Life's short. Even while
We talk Time, hateful, runs a mile.
Don't trust tomorrow's bough
For fruit. Pluck this, here, now.

Focusing on the here and now becomes more important for people who have lost, as does making changes in the ways they run their lives.

Lesson 2: Re-prioritising your life and goals

A major loss, an illness or death makes people more acutely aware of the shortness of time and the fragility of life. Some people may decide to cut back on the time they spend in jobs and on their careers, to spend more time with family and friends. Others may decide to pursue a new career or undertake an educational course they always had put off for the future. People talk of beginning to value time and their management of it more.

Ann, 43, who lost her 35-year-old brother to AIDS says,

'I think I'm much more conscious of life around me, where people are with their lives and where they're going. Since Wayne died I believe you have to be very conscious of what you're doing and where you're going. I went through the whole thing with him and although it was terrible, it was great also. We said our good-byes and one of the last things he said was 'Always do what's right for you.' I feel very empowered by those words.'

Ann's comments summarise that feeling so many people speak about –

examining your life and goals and re-evaluating what is important – and right for you. For some people, this takes the form of being more adventurous. Perhaps they have never pushed themselves to the limit nor taken risks. Loss and grief can make us better risk-takers.

We begin to realise that life holds dangers as well as rewards. Linked to this sense of adventure is a healthy curiosity. Curiosity about the world works against complacency and stagnation. When we are curious about the world, we tend to push our boundaries. By challenging ourselves in this way, we constantly expand our ability to perceive things from different points of view.

Maria McCarthy says of these challenges to life's goals,

'Priorities change. Life is now changed for me. You look at things differently.'

Joel, 44, whose mother died of brain cancer says,

'I watched my mother suffer, I saw the state she was in. It was very traumatic. But, the experience gave me some insights. I started my goal to live as completely every day of your life that you have left. I don't want to fall into any complacency about life. If I want to do something – I'll do it.'

In re-evaluating their priorities and life goals, people often speak about a new search for simplicity. It is only after something has been taken from us that we realise its true value. Most of us spend a lot of energy in life taking care of details of living that appear important, but perhaps get in the way of life's small but important moments and interactions.

One woman who was widowed at 42, bemoaned the fact that most of her married life she had 'wasted' time doing her housework and prodding her reluctant husband to keep the house tidy. Now, she said, it didn't matter how the house looked. She realised she had been obsessive about the house, and as she said, *'It's now hard to fathom why.'* She wished she had spent more time relaxing, enjoying herself and the relationship with her husband, rather than worrying about whether the kitchen was tidy or the living-room presentable. Grief teaches us that we need to simplify our lives. We need to de-clutter our lives of all the seemingly important things that can really wait. We need to spend time on the simpler joys of life.

Lesson 3: Becoming more sensitive and thoughtful

Many people talk about the positive changes in their personalities as a result of their loss experience. They say they have become more tolerant, more sensitive, more loving with others in their lives. Some people even describe becoming less controlling and willing to take life as it comes their way.

Arnold, 50, whose 74-year-old father died of pancreatic cancer says,

'This experience has worked to develop a softness in me. I have a greater sense of my vulnerable side. I don't have to be so in charge of things. I now have an inner peacefulness.'

Learning we can't necessarily control our lives, loss teaches us that life can't be hurried. Grief also teaches us that we must be patient with ourselves and others. We may learn to wait good humouredly for others who must catch up.

Maria McCarthy says of the changes in sensitivity she experienced,

'You're in a different place. I have more clarity, more awareness. I don't feel judgemental about things.'

Jerry, 52, found the changes he experienced very profound. He has developed a stronger sense of life and understanding the pain others are experiencing. He was very involved with his 76-year-old mother before she died of breast cancer. He says,

'She taught me to have appreciation for people who are sick and frail. Before her illness, I was impatient with people. I would see someone in a walker or a wheel-chair in a restaurant or an older person walking with a cane and I would think, 'Oh, come on, get out of my way.' My mother's illness gave me a sense of the importance of life, more compassion for people and an understanding of the pain that people go through.'

Like Jerry, many people talk about the love and empathy they now feel towards others. They often speak of their own awkwardness and discomfort when faced previously with someone who had experienced a loss. Now, they say, they understand and wish they had responded differently. Now, they say, when they meet someone who is grieving, they say they respond easily and differently from before. Some people go so far as to say that they know instantly when they are in the presence of someone who has experienced grief because there is more compassion, more understanding and more awareness of everything it means to have a loss among people who have experienced it.

After loss, people believe that there is magic in sharing themselves with someone else. They believe they have gained strength and competencies they did not realise they had.

Lesson 4 : Realising personal strength and competence

Many people who have experienced life-threatening and life-changing illness and loss speak about discovering strengths and competencies in themselves that surprised them. Those who have been care-givers to loved ones before their loved ones had died describe engaging in activities that they never would have believed they could do. People, often to their surprise, find they can provide nursing care, be assertive in talking to doctors and in doing battle with hospitals and insurance companies.

Melissa, 41, whose 45-year-old husband, Gary died of lung cancer says,

'Watching Gary die was horrible. But I got something from all that. I would say that 'sacrifice' is the world that comes to mind in the last two years of his life. Sacrificing so much of myself. I learned a lot from that. I learned how much I can put up with. I feel stronger for it. I learned that there's nothing to be feared in life. There's nothing I couldn't do.'

Melissa was surprised that she could do so much, as she says, make so many 'sacrifices', and be stronger for it. Another woman, Gayle, 38, whose husband died of colon cancer says,

'If you'd asked me 10 years ago – no, make that two years ago, whether I could do this, I would have said, 'Not on your life!'. But it's amazing what you can do when you have to. I went from being a workaholic to being available to people in my life. I did things I never imagined I could do – for my husband, for my children, for the rest of his family. Part of me didn't know I had the strength for this. Sometimes I still find it amazing.'

Finding strength, being amazed by your own competencies and resilience are themes that are told again and again by people who have learned from loss.

Maria McCarthy summarises this well in her comment.

'I didn't know I had such resilience.'

A major loss brings into focus not only aspects of your own capabilities, but also, the importance of sharing and connecting with others.

Lesson 5: Realising the importance of relationships

Losing an important person can shatter your assumptions that there will always be time to express your love to family and friends, to share your thoughts and dreams and memories. It makes you question whether you shouldn't work harder at doing things together, to simply be together.

Loss and grief teach us that relationships can never be taken for granted. Relationships can bring tremendous satisfaction and we now fully realise their worth. Yes, there is a risk in loving, but love also enriches us in a fullness of life.

Maria McCarthy's words echo the value of relationships in life,

'The accident brought sharply into focus what's important in life. ...I would walk over coals for my partner. You meet some people in life who make a difference.'

It's valuing these people who do make a difference that enriches our lives after loss. Our understanding of the importance of relationships has the potential to enrich all the relationships we currently have – or will develop.

Robyn, 32, whose sister died of breast cancer says,

'I learned that when you love someone, the relationship is so important. This experience of grief has enhanced my relationship with other people because I realise that time is so important.'

People speak about how they now value others in their lives, the time they spend with these people, like they never valued them before. Many people say that they attempt to make more time for others – friends and even

201

strangers in need. They try to be more positive and constructive in their relationships with others. Most importantly, they are no longer afraid of expressing openly the love and affection they have for family and friends.

This 'having more time' for relationships is related to another lesson – that of resolving conflicts.

Lesson 6: Resolving conflicts

With a major loss, we can learn the benefits of resolving conflicts in our relationships. Unfinished business can be negative and destructive in our lives. In families where conflicts after loss are confronted and resolved, individual members of the family speak of the great relief they feel. The burden of conflict and the relief that can be achieved if you confront any unfinished business can be very liberating.

Genie, 45, whose 78-year-old mother died of pancreatic cancer says,

> 'I learned to forgive. I understood how important that was. I didn't want to have that 'I wish I had' guilt. My mum stopped drinking during the last years of her life and I came to know her in a way I was unable to when I was growing up. Towards the end, I learned a lot about the reasons why my parents did some of the things they did, felt some of the ways they felt and acted some of the ways they acted. I forgave her everything.'

Lessons about the emotional advantages of resolving conflicts and liberating ourselves from the burden of unfinished business can be applied to many of our other relationships in life. Our learning can be transferred from one context of our lives to another.

Lesson 7: Losing a fear of death

Many people who experience a loved one's death and cope with that loss, find their fear of death erased by that experience. Some people are surprised that they no longer see death as frightening or horrible. Fear has been replaced by the intrigue and mystery of death. People say they are more peaceful about future deaths – including their own.

Thomas, 35, whose partner died of AIDS says,

'Death is part of life, but we don't talk about it. We often try not to think about it, it's become such a taboo. I think most of us are unprepared for it. I think we need to talk about it more – even teach classes about it – to make it less frightening. I think part of the reason we are so frightened is because we know so little about it. Watching Robert die, seeing him get closer and closer to death took a lot of fear away from me. The process was terrible, yet it wasn't terrible. He knew he was dying and came to accept it. He had such dignity. I'm not fearful of death. Tell others how much you love and appreciate them. I embrace life more now.'

Finding new meaning in life, embracing that life and developing a worldview that finds positive elements in the tragedy of loss often strengthens people's religious or spiritual beliefs.

Lesson 8: Finding a spiritual dimension

It is not always those people who are religious or spiritual who find a deeper meaning in loss. Loss brings with it the potential for everyone to find a spiritual dimension in their experience. Some people report that the loss had led them to question – often severely – their religious and spiritual beliefs. However, in the final analysis, most of these people found that their faith helped them better able to find meaning or make sense of the loss.

Thomas, for example says,

'I experienced very much a great comfort in my faith. I felt a deepening awareness of what I had spiritually. It was a comfort. And my faith helped me through the tough times. There were moments when I questioned life, death, fate, faith – everything – but finally for me, my faith was reinforced. I don't think you can go through something like this and not believe in some higher force – and gain meaning from the experience.'

Spiritual awareness and spiritual growth means something different for all of us. Having faith takes effort. Certainly during the days of your grief there have been times when you have despaired and felt spiritually deserted, rejected and shamed by your loss. Finding a spiritual connection, a faith in the mystery of life helps the healing process. By finding a spiritual dimension in your experience – whatever that might mean for you – you can hope to find connection to serenity. Difficult times pull our energy inward and encourage us to search for faith and serenity.

A NOTE ABOUT OUR LESSONS

Being more aware of yourself, feeling more alive in the world, becoming more adventurous, curious yet patient, being more compassionate, feeling more spiritually connected, are very powerful lessons.

Our lessons help us to cope with the loss and transform us in our new lives. By reflecting on the painful experience of our griefs, we realise they have made us wiser. We can learn a lot at the low tide of life. Our sorrow heightens our joy, our depression heightens our laughter and we now know that if it weren't for our low times, we wouldn't recognise the peaks.

PROMPT FOR YOUR PEN

Exercise   **Reflecting on your lessons of loss**

Reflect on your experiences of loss and grief. What lessons did you learn?
How have these lessons changed your life?
If you had to choose one significant lesson to share with others, what would it be?

Joyce Wadler writes humourously and sensitively about her lessons of loss. Her concluding paragraphs in her book, ***My Breast: One Woman's Cancer Story***, pithily convey the insights she gained,

> 'Nothing is real until you are close to it, and for a few weeks I was given something few people have: a dress rehearsal of my mortality. And, while it has not made me a model of mental health, though I remain tempted by the drama and dangers of espionage agents and ladies' men, it changed me. Death, I now see, may not come when I am eighty-five and weary, or after I have solved all my problems or met all my deadlines. It will come whenever it damn well pleases. All I can control – for whatever fight I put up should a cancer make

a comeback – is the time between. So when I see something I want, I grab it. If the tulips are particularly yellow, I buy them. If Pavarotti is in town, I make a run to the Met and work the crowd for a scalper. I make time for my friends the way I used to make time for work. If someone treats me disrespectfully, I leave.

As for the mark on my left breast, I am happy to have it. It is the battle scar over my heart; and if no one but my doctor and the girls at the gym have seen it lately, I am certain, believing as I do in musical comedies, that somebody will soon.

"So how'd ya get that?" he'll ask, our first lazy morning, and I'll say, delighted he has found me, "Glad you asked, 'cause it's a wonderful story...".

AND IN CONCLUSION...

Sometimes grief-work appears to be endless. After someone we care about dies or we experience a major loss, knowing how to go on is difficult. Grief-work brings with it the choice to heal. Grief-work requires us to dig deep into our souls and resolve to forge ahead.

Loss calls into question one's existence. Loss calls into question our purpose in life. Loss calls into question one's truths. In order to heal, we must search for new truths.

When you are feeling victimised and looking at life as capricious and unpredictable, it may be hard to find the positive lessons. By finding something positive in your loss you can enhance your self-esteem and your sense of the world as a place where we are challenged and we need to find constructive ways of dealing with those challenges.

From loss to gain, the journey is a worthwhile one and our lessons of loss help to transform us.

NOTES